THE BIBLE IN THE CONTEMPORARY WORLD

The Bible in the Contemporary World

*Exploring texts and
contexts – then and now*

Richard Bauckham

Also published in the United States of America in 2016
as *The Bible in the Contemporary World: Hermeneutical ventures*
by William B. Eerdmans, Grand Rapids, Michigan

First published in Great Britain in 2016

Society for Promoting Christian Knowledge
36 Causton Street
London SW1P 4ST
www.spck.org.uk

British Library Cataloguing-in-Publication Data
A catalogue record for this book is available from the British Library

ISBN 978–0–281–07484–6
eBook ISBN 978–0–281–07485–3

Typeset by Graphicraft Limited, Hong Kong
First printed in Great Britain by Ashford Colour Press
Subsequently digitally printed in Great Britain

eBook by Graphicraft Limited, Hong Kong

Produced on paper from sustainable forests

Contents

CONTENTS

Acknowledgments

The author and publisher are grateful for permission to reproduce material from the following sources, in some cases with revision by the author.

"Reading Scripture as a Coherent Story," in *The Art of Reading Scripture,* ed. Ellen F. Davis and Richard B. Hays (Grand Rapids: Eerdmans, 2003), 38-53.

"Are We Still Missing the Elephant? C. S. Lewis's 'Fernseed and Elephants' Half a Century On," *Theology* 116 (2013): 427-34. Used by permission of SPCK.

"Contemporary Western Culture — A Biblical-Christian Critique," published as "The Bible in Mission: The Modern/Postmodern Context," in *The Bible in Mission,* ed. Pauline Hoggarth, Fergus Macdonald, Bill Mitchell, and Knud Jørgensen, Regnum Edinburgh Centenary Series 18 (Oxford: Regnum, 2013), 43-55. Used by permission.

"The Bible and Globalization," in *The Gospel and Globalization: Exploring the Religious Roots of a Globalized World,* ed. Michael W. Goheen and Erin G. Glanville (Vancouver: Regent College Publishing/Geneva Society, 2009), 27-48. Used by permission.

"Freedom and Belonging," *Christian Reflections* 39 (2011): 11-18. Used by permission.

"Humans, Animals, and the Environment in Genesis 1-3," in *Genesis and Christian Theology,* ed. Nathan MacDonald, Mark W. Elliott, and Grant Macaskill (Grand Rapids: Eerdmans, 2012), 175-89.

"The Story of the Earth according to Paul," *Review and Expositor* 108 (2011): 91-97.

"Ecological Hope in Crisis?" *Anvil* 30 (2014): 43-54. Used by permission of Hendrickson.

"God's Embrace of Suffering," published as "The Cross and God's Embrace of Suffering," in *Atonement as Gift,* ed. Katie Heffelfinger and Patrick McGlinchey (Milton Keynes, U.K.: Paternoster, 2014).

"Where Is Wisdom to Be Found? Christ and Wisdom in Colossians," published as "Where Is Wisdom to Be Found? Colossians 1.15-20 (2)," in *Reading Texts, Seeking Wisdom,* ed. David F. Ford and Graham Stanton (London: SCM, 2003), 129-38. Used by permission.

Introduction

The fourteen essays in this volume were first written for a wide variety of contexts over a period of more than a decade. But reading through them again now I see that they do represent in a coherent and consistent way an approach to the Bible and to the contemporary world that I have developed over a long period. They stem from my long-standing and strong conviction that part of the responsibility of a Christian interpreter of Scripture today is to try to understand our contemporary context and to explore the Bible's relevance to it in ways that reflect serious critical engagement with that context. As I have sometimes said to students, in order to relate the Bible to the contemporary world we need both an interpretation of Scripture and an interpretation of the contemporary world. We cannot just repeat what our predecessors said to very different contexts in the past. We need to find the points of challenging interplay between the Bible and our own context. Too many Christian attempts to open up the Bible's relevance today or to draw on the resources of the Bible in order to address the contemporary world lack this crucial element of contextuality.

My engagements with contemporary society in this volume largely relate to the contemporary West, the context I know best, but I am constantly aware of the relationship between the West and the rest of the world, as, for example, in globalization (chapter 4) and in anthropogenic climate change. This is the more so because, in my view, any biblical-Christian critique of the contemporary world must prioritize the interests of the poor, both in the affluent societies of the West and in the rest of the world, especially at a time when the gap between rich and poor continues to grow, both globally and locally.

Some of the essays address global and unprecedented features of our contemporary context: globalization and ecological destruction (including, but by no means limited to, the effects of climate change). These could be seen as tests of the Bible's potential to speak relevantly to the distinctive context of our times. A key aspect of the way I bring the biblical texts into relationship with these contemporary realities is by means of the notion of metanarrative (a term that, as I explain in chapter 1, I use in a rather broader sense than that which was first given it in French postmodernist use). A metanarrative is a story about the whole of reality — or at least about the whole of human history — providing the meaning and purpose by which people and societies can live in relation to that whole.

The Bible's metanarrative is the story of God and the world, from creation to new creation, in which God's purpose for the world takes effect in the blessing and salvation and fulfillment of the world as his cherished creation. I have said "God and the world," but in our contemporary context of ecological crisis it is essential to fill that out as "God and humans and the rest of creation." The story is of a three-way interrelationship among these three participants. If we live, as humans have since the time things first went wrong, in a time of crisis in the human relationship to God, in our own time especially that crisis is inseparable from the crisis in the human relationship with the rest of creation. God's redemptive purpose is to heal both these painfully fractured relationships, and he certainly cannot fully heal one without in the same process healing the other.

This becomes clear if we read the crucial opening chapters of the Bible (Genesis 1–3) in terms of this threefold pattern of relationships and with an openness to the ecological realities of our time. Then the message of these chapters, on which all too many contemporary Christians focus for entirely wrong reasons, becomes powerfully relevant (see especially chapter 6). But as well as the beginning of the biblical metanarrative we need also the story of God's decisive redemptive acts, in the story of Jesus, and the hope for the cosmic (not merely individual or even merely human) future that arises out of them (see especially chapters 7, 8, 10, 13). Christian hope, founded especially on the cross and resurrection of Jesus, is decisive both for orientating and sustaining Christian hopeful action in the world, but it can also become problematic in situations in which realistic possibilities of hope seem to be running out. I explore this issue in relation to the ecological crisis in chapter eight.

Any attempt to retrieve the biblical metanarrative in its relevance for our contemporary world must take pains to distinguish it from the modern narrative of the post-Enlightenment West (and derivatively of much of the rest of the world) with which it has, in the modern period, too often been entangled. (See especially chapters 1 and 3 for the characteristics that distinguish the "nonmodern" metanarrative of the Bible from the modern metanarrative of progress.) For the modern world has itself developed under the guiding hand of its own metanarrative, which is still a major influence in our contemporary situation. This narrative of progressive mastery over the world and emancipation from nature is the one that gave rise to the ecological problems of today, while in its economic version it is still a powerful ideology of free-market economics and globalization.

Since the days when it had become almost a cliché, in both Christian and wider cultural discussion, to claim that contemporary Western culture was moving decisively out of modernity into postmodernity, the issue of the modern and the postmodern has become more problematic (see chapter 3). It is clear that, despite the blows that the metanarrative of modernity has suffered over the past century, it is still a powerful force, especially in its economic form. This form, with its materialistic conviction that economic growth is the supreme good on which all other goods in life depend and to which all other goals must be subordinated, is a peculiarly debased version of the Enlightenment narrative of progress, but it has our Western societies, with their hedonism and addiction to excess, in its idolatrous grip. Postmodernism has proved impotent to resist it and in fact has readily adapted to it. Our culture is currently a fluid mixture of modern and postmodern features, which we misunderstand unless we give full recognition to both. For many young people in Western culture today these disparate features together form a worldview that works for them.

The most important feature of postmodernism, in the context of the arguments pursued in this book, is its critique of the modern metanarratives of rational mastery and progress, and in this respect it may assist a Christian critique. But postmodernism is certainly not the wholly supportive ally of Christian faith that some Christian thinkers have optimistically supposed. Its tendency to radical fragmentation of life and its deconstructive critique of any claims to universal truth are challenges that Christians must take up without simply reverting to Enlightenment rationalism (see chapter 14). Especially important for my thinking in this book is the question of whether the biblical metanarrative is vulnerable to the postmodern critique of the modern metanarratives. Taking up the postmodern challenge in this respect is salutary and fruitful for clarifying features of the biblical metanarrative that modern Christian attempts to assimilate it to the myth of progress ignored or played down (see chapter 1).

I have long thought that the understanding of human freedom must lie close to the heart of any fruitful Christian engagement with contemporary western culture.[1] It seems to me an issue with which Christians have so far failed to come to grips, despite some use of such attractive but ambiguous terms as liberation. A notion of freedom as freedom from all limits, which began to take shape as early as the Renaissance, has spawned a variety of key features of our contemporary world, including its hyperindividualism, its consumerism, its excessive suspicion of all authority, its alienation from nature, the atomization of urban life and the problem of chronic loneliness, even the rejection of God. Freedom has trumped goodness as a supreme value. Freedom *from* has usurped the more important value of freedom *for*. An understanding of freedom that is incompatible with limits or belonging has sacrificed relationships and contentment to ludicrously unrealistic dreams of individual fulfillment (see chapters 3 and 5).

The nature of these essays means that the account and the critique of contemporary Western society that they offer is piecemeal, not comprehensive or balanced. Some readers may find it too negative. I believe that Christians are called to undertake a countercultural and prophetic role because they are unusually equipped to do so, having available to them a viewpoint from outside the cultural consensus, a viewpoint from which they can exercise critical discernment in assessing the goods and the evils of our world. It is a viewpoint that requires their solidarity with all who are excluded from the dominant culture, and it is a viewpoint that requires costly setting aside of their own self-interest. But every human culture or society is a mixture of good and evil; each has its strengths and its weaknesses. Christians should celebrate the positive achievements and life-affirming values of the societies in which they participate and to which they should contribute. There is not very much of that in this volume and, were it pretending to some kind of balanced and comprehensive overview, that would be a serious weakness. But it makes no such claim. Those essays that engage in critique of the contemporary world simply aim to identify points at which the trends of our time clash with the direction of God's purpose for the good of his creation, as the Bible delineates it.

Since these essays were written as independent essays for a variety of contexts, there is no right order in which to read them. The best way

---

1. See my earlier collection of essays: *God and the Crisis of Freedom: Biblical and Contemporary Perspectives* (Louisville: Westminster John Knox, 2002).

to read a book of this kind is to start with whichever chapters make the strongest immediate appeal.

In this introduction I have tried to sketch some of the principles, concerns, and themes that give coherence and consistency to the varied essays in this book. I hope this will give readers a context within which to appreciate the specific contributions of each chapter. But I also hope I have not made the arguments of the various chapters too predictable. I anticipate that readers who enjoy surprises, as I do, will also find some of those. After all, the Bible itself is full of surprises. Just as we think we have got its messages all neatly tied up in a portable parcel, we find it saying something that doesn't fit in the parcel we have made for it and breaks out. Such biblical surprises should also be part of the Bible's relevance to the contemporary world.

CHAPTER 1

Reading Scripture as a Coherent Story

The church's reading of Scripture has usually presupposed its narrative unity, that is, that the whole of the Bible — or the Bible read as a whole — tells a coherent story. Any part of Scripture contributes to or illuminates in some way this one story, which is the story of God's purpose for the world. If Scripture does indeed tell the story of God's purpose for the world, then we should certainly expect to find unity and coherence in it. But the idea of reading Scripture as a unified narrative seems problematic from at least two very different perspectives: that of biblical scholars for whom the great diversity of the biblical texts makes it inappropriate to the nature of the Bible and that of postmodern critics for whom a unified narrative would constitute Christianity the oppressive metanarrative that historically it has at least very often been.[1] This essay begins with a section responding mainly to the first concern. The argument about the Bible is then interrupted by a critical consideration of the postmodern critique of metanarratives in order to resume, in the third section, a discussion of the biblical story with some conceptual tools provided by the postmodern approach.

1. The Biblical Story — Unity and Diversity

We should first be clear about the senses in which Scripture is clearly not a unified narrative. (1) Not all Scripture is narrative. Those books that are

---

1. There is a third perspective the paper does not address: that of Jews for whom the Christian reading of the two testaments as a unified narrative is problematic.

in narrative form sometimes contain nonnarrative material within the narrative context (e.g., law in Exodus-Deuteronomy), and it is not difficult to see how some nonnarrative books can be seen as implicitly, by their canonical relationship to the narrative works, given a narrative setting within the story told by the narrative books (e.g., Psalms, Lamentations). In a sense this is true of the largest category of nonnarrative works in each testament: prophecy and apostolic letters. (In the case of the former, the Hebrew Bible recognizes this in calling the historical books from Joshua to 2 Kings "'the Former Prophets" and the prophetic books "the Latter Prophets.") Prophecy and apostolic letters are intrinsically related to the biblical story, to which they constantly refer, even summarizing and retelling parts of it. The biblical narrative of God, his people, and the world structures their theology and is presupposed in the way they address the present and future. The apocalypses — Daniel and Revelation — like parts of the prophets, presuppose "the story so far" in envisioning its eschatological conclusion. Thus, while not all Scripture is generically narrative, it can reasonably be claimed that the story Scripture tells, from creation to new creation, is the unifying element that holds literature of other genres together with narrative in an intelligible whole. However, there are a few books of which this is more difficult to say: Song of Songs, Proverbs, Ecclesiastes. Association with Solomon links them externally to the story of Israel, but they seem to lack intrinsic connection with it.[2] The presence of these books in the canon might suggest that Scripture finds its unity not in the story it tells but in the God about whom it speaks (though the problem of a book that does not speak of God at all — the Song of Songs — would still remain). But this is not a convincing distinction, since Scripture in general knows who God is from the story of God, his people, and the world that it tells. The solution surely lies in recognizing that, although this story focuses on the particularity of God's activity in history, it also, especially in its beginning (Genesis 1–11), recognizes God's general relationship as sovereign Creator to the whole creation and all people. In any case, it is important to note, with the trend of scholarship since the demise of the biblical theology movement, that the shape of the canon is distorted if biblical theology focuses on salvation history either at the expense of the

2. But note the way Ellen Davis finds that the imagery of the Song of Songs links it with significant parts of the Old Testament story: Ellen F. Davis, *Proverbs, Ecclesiastes, and the Song of Songs*, Westminster Bible Companion (Louisville: Westminster John Knox, 2000).

wisdom literature of the Old Testament or at the expense of the significance of creation throughout the canon.

(2) The Bible does not tell a single story in the way that either a novel or a modern work of historiography by a single author may. Whatever unity it has is not the kind of coherence that a single author can give his or her work. The narrative books in fact adopt a wide variety of kinds of storytelling and historiography, while the future completion of the story can naturally only be indicated by quite different narrative means than those which tell, in whatever way, a story set in the past. Moreover, no one before the final editors or compilers of the New Testament canon ever planned the assembling of precisely this collection of works. Of course, Christians believe that God's Spirit inspired these books and God's providence guided their collection, but this does not warrant our supposing the Bible must have the kind of unity a human author can give to a work. God's inspiration has evidently not suppressed the human diversity of the many human minds and circumstances that, at the human level, have constituted Scripture the collection of very varied materials that it is. Perhaps one could appeal to Mikhail Bakhtin's notion of the polyphonic novel, in which the voices of the various characters and even the narrator are autonomous and equal.[3] The unity of such a novel consists in the dialogue of conflicting voices. Perhaps the relation of the author to a polyphonic novel might constitute a kind of analogy for the relation of God to Scripture, but it would remain an analogy. Scripture has neither the *kind* of diversity nor the *kind* of unity a polyphonic novel does.

While the Bible does not have the kind of unity and coherence a single human author can give a literary work, there is nevertheless a remarkable extent to which the biblical texts themselves recognize and assert, in a necessarily cumulative manner, the unity of the story they tell. The books from Genesis to 2 Kings constitute a single edited history from creation to the exile, though the editors, especially of the Pentateuch, were evidently content to let a good deal of variety in the traditions they incorporated stand. In this they form something of a model for the compilers of the canon itself. 1-2 Chronicles spans the same period as Genesis–2 Kings, in its first eight chapters employing genealogy as a quite sophisticated means

---

3. See Sue Vice, *Introducing Bakhtin* (Manchester: Manchester University Press, 1997), chap. 3. One of Bakhtin's major examples of the polyphonic novel was Dostoevsky's *The Brothers Karamazov,* but whether he was correct in regarding the various voices in the novel as equal is debatable. The issue bears some resemblance to debates about unity and diversity in the Bible.

of representing the history from Adam to David. Although Ezra-Nehemiah is not placed after 1-2 Chronicles in the Hebrew canon, the editorial replication of the opening verses of Ezra at the end of 2 Chronicles does create a link, indicating the continuation of the same story. As well as these two parallel narratives, stretching from creation to, in one case, the exile, in the other, the reconstitution after the exile, the Old Testament contains the three short stories: Ruth, Esther, and Jonah.[4] Each gives a perspective significantly different from those represented within the two major narrative sequences, but this is only possible because each is explicitly linked to the larger story of Israel (Ruth 1:1; 4:17-22; Esth. 2:5-6; Jon. 1:1 with 2 Kings 14:25).

The one biblical book that, in its way, matches the span of the whole canon is the Gospel of John, which begins with a deliberate echo of the opening words of Genesis (1:1: "In the beginning") and concludes with a reference to the parousia ("until I come" [21:23], Jesus' last words and the last words of the Gospel before the colophon [21:24-25]) that corresponds to the prayer with which Revelation concludes (22:20: "Come, Lord Jesus!"). Matthew's opening genealogy resumes the whole Old Testament history from Abraham onward, at the same time evoking the messianic promises to Abraham and David, while the Gospel ends with reference to "the end of the age" (28:20). (It is worth noting that, whereas the biblical narratives in general leave a chronological gap between Old and New Testament stories [even if the deuterocanonical books of Maccabees are taken into account], the two genealogies of Matthew and Luke do create a kind of narrative link across this gap.) Throughout the New Testament, of course, the story of Jesus is treated as the continuation of the story of Israel and as initiating the fulfillment of the prophetic promises to Israel.

A sense of the unity of the biblical story is also given by a number of summaries to be found in both testaments, though there is no summary of the whole story from creation to new creation. Summaries of the story of Israel, of varying scope, include:

Deuteronomy 6:20-24 (exodus to occupation of the land);
Deuteronomy 26:5-9 (settlement in Egypt to occupation of the land);
Joshua 24:2-13 (Abraham to occupation of the land);
Nehemiah 9:6-37 (creation + Abraham to return from exile);

---

4. Jonah appears among the Twelve Prophets in all canonical orders, but it clearly differs generically from the other components of the Twelve.

Psalm 78 (exodus to David);
Psalm 105 (Abraham to occupation of the land);
Psalm 106 = 1 Chronicles 16:8-16 (exodus to exile);
Psalm 135:8-12 (exodus to occupation of the land);
Psalm 136 (creation + exodus to occupation of the land);
Acts 7:2-50 (Abraham to Solomon).

Different as the focus and intent of these various summaries are, they tend to highlight the same major landmarks of the story. Just one of them virtually summarizes the whole Old Testament story: Nehemiah 9:6-37, placed at the chronological end of that story, resumes the whole story from creation to its own time. Rather surprisingly, the Bible contains only one summary of the Old and New Testament stories as one: Acts 13:17-41 begins with the patriarchs and ends with the resurrection of Jesus and the preaching of the apostolic message. The New Testament contains many, mostly very short, summaries of the story of Jesus, some of them, like the later creeds of the church, projecting the story to its future end at his parousia (e.g., Acts 10:36-43). Despite such anticipations of the end of the story, it is important to notice that all these summaries are *situated* within the biblical story. Scripture does not and could not summarize its story from a standpoint outside the story, which is unfinished. The summaries are themselves part of the story and even contribute to the story's own development.

Among ways in which the canonical texts themselves assert their unity, we should also mention the book of Revelation, which I have elsewhere described as "the climax of prophecy"[5] because it presents itself as the summation of the whole biblical tradition of prophecy, not least in its prolific allusion to a large range of Old Testament prophetic texts whose continuing surplus of eschatological reference it affirms and interprets. As a prophetic text, Revelation offers in some sense an overview of the story from the perspective of its end, but even here the end is anticipated from within the still continuing story.

In these and other ways, it can be seen not to be alien to the biblical texts themselves, read as a cumulative whole, to seek a unitary story encompassing the whole. For a warrant to do this, we do not need to rely solely on the mere existence of the canon or the church's tradition of read-

5. Richard Bauckham, *The Climax of Prophecy: Studies on the Book of Revelation* (Edinburgh: T&T Clark, 1993).

ing it,[6] nor need we make a simply arbitrary decision to read Scripture in this way, but can appeal to significant features of the texts in themselves. At the same time, however, we must recognize that the unity of the story cannot be a simple one handed to us on a canonical plate. The narratives are told from various junctures within the story and from a variety of perspectives. In the Old Testament we have something like a master version of the main story up to the exile (Genesis–2 Kings), but we also have diverse rereadings of it and interactions with it in the Prophets, a significantly different retelling of it in 1-2 Chronicles, tangential narratives that seem to offer corrective angles on it (Ruth, Esther, Jonah), and books that challenge essential features of its theology (Job, Ecclesiastes). In the New Testament we have fresh and diverse rereadings of the Old Testament story (e.g., Paul and James on Abraham), while the Gospel story of Jesus is told in no less than four different versions in the Gospels, along with comment and interpretation in Paul, Hebrews, 1 Peter, Revelation. The fourfold Gospel is the most obvious and telling example of diverse renderings of the biblical story, but the other instances we have mentioned show that it is not a unique feature of Jesus' story but of a piece with the general character of Scripture.

At this point it may be useful to remember the distinction the narratologist Gérard Genette makes between story and narrative.[7] A literary narrative may differ in many ways from the story it tells (whether the story is construed as fictional or true). For example, the order in which events are narrated may differ from the order in which they occur in the story. A narrative need not narrate all the events of the story, while some events may be narrated a number of times, from different points of view (whether of characters or narrators), from different temporal points in the story, conveying different information, highlighting different aspects of significance. This important distinction between story and narrative may help us to see that the plurality of narratives in Scripture — such that many recount the same events differently and none tells the whole story — is not in principle an obstacle to seeking in the Bible a single coherent story that all the narratives together tell and each partially tells.

---

6. I am less happy than Gerard Loughlin, *Telling God's Story* (Cambridge: Cambridge University Press, 1996), pp. 46-51, to rely on the church's "traditional reading rules" (doctrines) for reading Scripture as a unity, without also seeking what there is about Scripture that makes such rules appropriate.

7. Loughlin, *Telling God's Story,* 52-62, summarizing the account in Gérard Genette, *Narrative Discourse,* trans. Jane E. Lewin (Oxford: Blackwell, 1980).

It is important also to recognize that the diversity of biblical renderings of the biblical story is distinctly limited, as comparison with, for example, other versions of the Old Testament story in texts among the Dead Sea Scrolls or the versions of the Gospel story to be found in the Gnostic Gospels from Nag Hammadi, readily shows. The Gospel of John tells recognizably the same story as the Synoptics, whereas the Gnostic Gospels do not. Partly because of specialization and the narrowing of horizons it entails, much recent scholarship has tended to exaggerate biblical diversity. Nevertheless, the diversity is such that readers of Scripture have their own work to do discerning the unity of the story. Moreover, the diversity of different versions of the story is not the only feature of Scripture that requires this. The sheer profusion of narrative materials in Scripture — the proliferation of little stories within the larger ones, the narrative directions left unfinished, the narrative hints that enlist readers' imagination, the ambiguity of stories that leave their meaning open, the narrative fragments of the stories of prophets in their books or of writers and churches in the apostolic letters, the very different kinds of narrative that resist division into simple alternatives such as "history" and "myth" or "fiction," the references to stories external to Scripture — even apart from the bearing of the nonnarrative literature on the narrative, makes any sort of finality in summarizing the biblical story inconceivable. Summaries are more or less essential, which is why we find them, as we have seen, in Scripture itself and why the creeds of the early church feature them prominently, but in neither case does just one summary emerge preeminent. Essential elements in a summary would not be hard to list. But the summaries cannot replace what they summarize; the story they summarize resists closure. The church must be constantly retelling the story, never losing sight of the landmark events, never losing touch with the main lines of theological meaning in the Scripture's own tellings and commentaries, but also open to the never-exhausted potential of the texts in their resonances with contemporary life.

There are perhaps two ways of understanding what is going on in retellings of the story, both within and beyond Scripture. One, located at the fashionable confluence of midrash and the postmodern, would understand it in terms of intertextuality. Texts are constantly being reinterpreted. There is obvious truth in this, but if it is the whole truth, if there is nothing outside the texts, the story risks being subject to the interests and designs — or mere intellectual playfulness — of its interpreters. Another approach (consistent with Genette's distinction between story and narrative) is to recognize that, while the telling of a story can be true, it can never be adequate to or exhaustive of the reality it renders. In this case, the fact that versions and interpretations multiply especially in the case of the story of Jesus is testimony to the importance of not reducing his reality to the limitations of a single rendering. The existence of the four Gospels, not to mention commentary in the apostolic letters, keeps readers aware that Jesus is neither captured in the text nor existent only as a textual construction but had and has his own reality to which the texts witness.

The considerations in this section have largely concerned formal characteristics of the biblical texts, rather than their material content. We have barely touched on what sort of a story it is the Bible tells. To discuss the coherence of the biblical story in terms of the content of its narratives requires a biblical theology, which obviously cannot be undertaken here. But some significant features of the biblical story will be discussed in section three, where they will be required to distinguish the biblical story from oppressive metanarratives of the kind that have suffered the critique of postmodern thinkers.

2. The Postmodern Critique of Metanarratives

The French philosopher Jean-François Lyotard[8] (d. 1998), in his *La condition postmoderne* (1979), famously and influentially defined the postmodern as incredulity toward grand narratives (or metanarratives — the terms are interchangeable).[9] He later thought this book put too much emphasis on the narrative form, since his target was comprehensive systems of explanation that do not necessarily take narrative form. Nevertheless it is noteworthy that not only the systems to which he was primarily referring, those of Hegel and Marx, but also most such systems in the modern period, including other versions of the idea of progress and scientistic accounts such as the currently popular elevation of Darwinism into a comprehensive explanation of human as well as other life, take narrative form. Even Platonism had a metanarrative. The term surely remains appropriate. Lyotard

8. My account of Lyotard on metanarratives is indebted to Steven Connor, *Postmodernist Culture: An Introduction to Theories of the Contemporary*, 2nd ed. (Oxford: Blackwell, 1997), pp. 23-43; Gary K. Browning, *Lyotard and the End of Grand Narratives* (Cardiff: University of Wales Press, 2000).

9. Jean-François Lyotard, *The Postmodern Condition*, trans. Geoff Bennington and Brian Massumi (Minneapolis: University of Minnesota Press, 1984), p. xxiv.

also later recognized that his own story of the obsolescence of all metanarratives in postmodernity was paradoxically itself a kind of metanarrative, at least in its absolutist claim to be the truth about history, and sought to avoid the idea of a historical succession of modernity followed by postmodernity. Whether he successfully resolved the paradox himself (arguably it is a version of the kind of paradox that relativism cannot avoid) is relatively unimportant, since the paradox has remained characteristic of much postmodern thinking that follows him in repudiating metanarratives.

Lyotard's rejection of grand narratives does not bear directly on the biblical or Christian story, though a consideration of the latter can certainly profit from attending to Lyotard's critique. It does not bear directly on the biblical or Christian story because its target is the project of modern reason that aspires to a comprehensive explanation of reality, including the human condition, and seeks thereby rationally based universal criteria by which to order society and to liberate humanity through technology. A metanarrative is a totalizing theory that aims to subsume all events, all perspectives, and all forms of knowledge in a comprehensive explanation. Lyotard's parade examples are the theories of Hegel and Marx.

This modern project presumes that reality, both nature and human history, is fundamentally comprehensible to reason. Lyotard's opposition to it involves a skeptical epistemology, which stresses the opacity of reality to reason, and a radical espousal of pluralism and heterogeneity against universality and unity. The contingency of events and the intractability of difference resist any totalizing theory. Metanarratives are necessarily authoritarian and oppressive, since they can subsume difference only by suppressing it. Lyotard's affirmation of difference is extreme. He opposes any universal values in theory and any attempt to reach consensus in society for the sake of a social order. The diverse language games of postmodern society are incommensurable and so plurality is irreducible. Order is always false and so oppressive. The centralized organization of society and cultural homogenization are features of the modern project and to be opposed. The only liberating kind of politics is agonistic, intensifying difference and so constantly resisting closure. The valorization of diversity and experimentation seems the only value and the right of the different to be heard the only justice, though both seem implicated in the relativist paradox.

The alleged incredulity toward metanarratives has a certain plausibility in contemporary Western society, but it can distract attention from the very powerful, late-modern grand narrative of consumerist individualism and free-market globalization, which aims to subsume precisely postmodern plurality. It appears liberating in its valorization of consumer lifestyle choices, but is oppressive in the much more realistic sense that affluent postmodern theorists are liable to ignore: it enriches the rich while leaving the poor poor, and it destroys the environment. In this way it continues the kind of oppression that the modern metanarratives of progress have always legitimated. It is hard to acquit much postmodern theory of unintentional or intentional collusion with this metanarrative. Postmodern relativism offers no cogent resistance to this metanarrative, which is not threatened by diversity so long as its overarching framework of alleged economic reality goes unchallenged.[10] Rather than the postmodern story of the end of metanarratives, we need a story that once again affirms universal values while resisting their co-option by the forces of domination. Terry Eagleton attempts a case for Marxism in this respect.[11] A case for the Christian story, which has been at least equally compromised by oppressive distortions and collusion with the modern myth of progress, may depend on a retrieval of aspects of the biblical story that resist its ideological distortions. Lyotard's extreme epistemological skepticism and indiscriminate valorization of difference as such are hardly attractive from a Christian perspective, but his critique of the modern grand narratives can still be instructive.

One does not have to go to Lyotard's extreme to see that the dream of modern reason, that it could fully capture and articulate reality, was an illusion. Theories of universal history that explain it in terms of a unidirectional movement of progress stand exposed as legitimations of the modern West's domination of the world.[12] Lyotard is right to stress the contingency of historical events and the intractability of reality to fully rational explanation and control. Global warming is a helpful illustration of the hugely powerful unintended consequences of the modern over-

10. Cf. Loughlin, *Telling God's Story*, pp. 30-32: "The delirium of free-market consumerism is made possible by the iron fist of capitalist technoscience that brooks no dissenters" (p. 31).

11. Terry Eagleton, *The Illusions of Postmodernism* (Oxford: Blackwell, 1996).

12. Felipe Fernández-Armesto's magnificent world history, *Civilizations* (London: Macmillan, 2000), shows by contrast how there is no single unifying and progressive story of civilization, such as the modern Eurocentric narratives embodied. Of course, this does not mean that stories can no longer be told about the development of civilizations. History does not dissolve into a merely random succession of change, as some postmodernism suggests. Fernández-Armesto speaks of process rather than progress (*Civilizations*, pp. 20-22). Experience is almost inescapably narrative, and we are bound to try to understand the past, as we do the present, by narrativizing it.

confidence in human mastery of nature and history. Auschwitz, of which Lyotard memorably said, "We wanted the progress of the mind, we got its shit,"[13] has rightly acquired the representative role of the surd that defeats any attempt at rational explanation of history. Totalizing metanarratives that entail closure do seem all too friendly to totalitarian politics.

3. The Biblical Story as a Nonmodern Metanarrative

The biblical story is not a metanarrative by Lyotard's definition, which limits the concept to a characteristically modern phenomenon, but I am not the first to extend the meaning and it seems useful to do so. One might properly call the biblical story a premodern metanarrative, were this not to appear to buy into the same sort of metanarrative about metanarratives that Lyotard himself sees lurking in the postmodern talk of the end of metanarratives. Such a meta-metanarrative remains in thrall to the modern metanarrative of progress, for which the label premodern is equivalent to obsolescent. But from the biblical story's own perspective its premodern origin is no bar to its contemporary truth or relevance. By calling the biblical story a nonmodern metanarrative I distinguish it from the modern metanarratives that Lyotard opposes. Consideration of the ways in which it is and is not what Lyotard defines and deplores will help to illuminate its character. This route to clarifying its character is particularly useful because there is a sense in which modern metanarratives are indebted to the Christian tradition and because the biblical story has been widely confused with them in the modern period.[14]

(1) What justifies the term *metanarrative* is that the biblical story is a story about the meaning of the whole of reality. Just as surely as it needs to be disentangled from the modern metanarratives of human rational mastery of nature and history, so it cannot be reduced to an unpretentious local language game in the pluralism of postmodernity. It makes a thoroughly universal claim, which combines the universality of the one Creator and Lord of all things with the particularity of this God's identification of himself as the God of Israel and of Jesus Christ. The latter gives it a particularity offensive to the modern metanarratives of universal reason and the former a universality even more offensive to postmodern relativism.

---

13. Quoted in Browning, *Lyotard*, p. 68.
14. The most fervent believers in the idea of progress I meet are often Christians.

The combination explains the way the biblical story combines "mythical" or symbolic narrative, especially and necessarily at its beginning and end, with particular historical narrative (which is not modern historiography, but historiography of one sort or another nevertheless). But even in this light, the way the main plot emerges from and often risks submersion or dissipation in the apparently redundant superfluity of little stories, as well as the already mentioned ambiguities and loose ends the complexity of the story entails, is quite remarkable. It says something about the status of particularity in the biblical story.

(2) Unlike the modern metanarratives, the biblical story does not account for history in terms of immanent reason or human mastery, but in terms of the freedom and purpose of God and of human freedom to obey or to resist God. There is a feature of typically modern narratives of all kinds (novels, films, etc.) that coheres strikingly with the modern meta-narratives: they are primarily about human achievement. Things happen to people, there are contingency and coincidence and meaningless tragedy, but on the whole the point lies in what people can make of these, how they can surmount disaster and achieve their freely chosen goals. These are the little stories that the metanarratives of rational mastery subsume without difficulty. By contrast, the protagonists of traditional stories (fairy stories, for example) are typically much more accepting of what happens to them and win (for of course they do win) by means of the assistance of nature or the favor of supernatural powers or just wildly improbable luck. Their world is more mysterious than comprehensible, and they do not expect to master it. In the biblical stories events are comprehensible insofar as God reveals his purposes and fulfills them. Human agency, of course, is important and celebrated where appropriate, but its success follows divine initiative and requires divine concurrence.

(3) In the biblical story there is therefore ample recognition of contingency in history, in the sense that much, perhaps most, that occurs is not the intended result of human activity. The carefully plotted stories of Joseph and Esther show how the providence of God prevails through chance, coincidence, and the unintended results of human activity (see Gen. 50:20), just as much as, though certainly also through, the obedient activity of servants of God. The biblical portrayal of divine providence cannot be equated with the immanent reason of history according to some modern metanarratives because it is contingent on the freedom of God and not open to rational calculation. So it invites trust, not mastery. God is to be trusted to be faithful to his promises, but he remains free in his fulfillment of them.

(4) In addition to the contingency in which biblical storytellers recognize the hand of God, there is a particular kind of intractability of history to comprehension even in these terms that appears, significantly, in surely the most dialectical aspect of biblical theology. In the Old Testament histories and prophets there is a strong tendency to recognize moral order in the world over which God is sovereign. Rulers and nations get what they deserve, and, although the God who is merciful as well as just may restrain his anger and remit punishment (i.e., the moral order includes grace as well as judgment), the opposite is not equally true; that is, righteousness is not normally rewarded with suffering. What the prophets and the historical books, from a salvation-historical perspective, assert about the fortunes of political societies, Proverbs, from a creational perspective, asserts of individual lives. In that sense Job's case is "counter-testimony"[15] against both Deuteronomistic history and so-called conventional wisdom. The trouble with Job's friends, however, is not so much that they endorse the tradition of observing moral order in God's world, rather that they do so in a spirit of dogmatic rationalism that cannot admit to a baffling exception, however obvious it might be. They exhibit the possible distortion of the biblical metanarrative into a rationalistic imposition of order that suppresses the real intractability of the evils of history. Job receives no explanation, only the assurance that because God is God he must in the end defeat evil, while Job because he is human cannot do so.[16] The mastery of nature and history remains the more certainly in God's hands, but the inscrutability of his ways, for which he will not be answerable to Job, is majestically asserted against the all too knowing dogmatism of the friends. Within the Old Testament it is Job above all that ensures the biblical story is not a comprehensive explanation of reality, even a divinely revealed one. Meaningless innocent suffering is the intractable surd in the story. The inclusion of Job in the canon is matched by the inclusion in the Psalter of the utterly bleak Psalm 88 with its painfully unanswered complaint.[17]

15. The term is Walter Brueggemann's, which he uses to characterize a variety of Old Testament texts that seem to oppose Israel's "core testimony" to YHWH: Walter Brueggemann, *Theology of the Old Testament* (Minneapolis: Fortress, 1997), part 2. I do not find all the material he adduces very convincingly placed in this category, but the dialectical model of a legal dispute involving testimony and counter-testimony helps to show how texts such as Job and Ecclesiastes make an essential contribution without overturning the "core testimony."

16. I read chapter 41 in this sense.

17. Note also, with Walter Brueggemann, *Abiding Astonishment: Psalms, Modernity*

Though Psalm 88 is the bleakest of the psalms of complaint, evincing scarcely any hope, others also voice the silence and absence of God in questions and complaints that remain unresolved. Even the terrible possibility that God has abrogated his covenant and will not be faithful to his promises is entertained (Ps 89:39; Lam 5:22). These psalms are by no means contradicting the testimony of the biblical story that God does act on behalf of the righteous. They presuppose it, in that it is only because of the belief that God does characteristically so act that they complain that he does not in their own case and insist that he must.[18] These psalms, therefore, and the people their inclusion in the Psalter encourages to pray them, live in dialectical tension with the testimony of Israel's story. This is perhaps a clue to the way the dying Jesus, in Matthew and Mark, makes his own the cry of desolation from the first verse of Psalm 22. The question arises precisely because God has so signally acted in the ministry of Jesus and promised the deliverance of his people through Jesus.

One could understand the lack of a "literature of dissent" in the New Testament, comparable with Job, Ecclesiastes, and the psalms of complaint in the Old Testament, by observing that the dialectic they create within the Old Testament story acquires centrality in the New Testament story through the Matthean and Markan rendering of the cross. But what does this imply for the continuing openness of the biblical story to unassimilable evil? The cross and resurrection of Jesus have been understood as an answer to the Old Testament's theodicy question, such that the psalms of complaint should no longer be prayed and Job's protest becomes redundant. In that case the biblical story, at its climax in Jesus, would achieve closure and the intractable evils of history and experience be overcome. However, the resurrection only anticipates eschatological closure. It bursts open the constraints of nature and history, promising an overwhelming good of a kind that will not, like any immanent theodicy, leave out the dead, the victims of history whose fate can never be justified by any product of history. Closure — meaning a finally satisfactory resolution of the problem of God's goodness in the world — is found in trust and hope, not in some explanation of the world that makes sense of evil, still less in the claim to human power to eradicate the evil human reason has understood.

(5) Although the matter cannot be explored here, we may note that,

---

and the Making of History (Louisville: Westminster John Knox, 1991), pp. 49-50, the texts Phyllis Trible called "texts of terror."

18. So Brueggemann, *Abiding Astonishment,* 52.

as well as the major dialectic within Scripture concerning moral order and incomprehensible evil, there are three other dialectics that the three Old Testament short stories serve to open up within the metanarrative: between androcentric and gynocentric perspectives on the story (Ruth),[19] between the evident activity of YHWH and his hidden providence (Esther), and between Israel's privilege and YHWH's concern for the nations (Jonah).

(6) In the biblical story it is rarely portrayed as the dominant metanarrative, but rather as up against the dominant narratives of the great empires from Pharaoh to Rome. Characteristically they proclaimed their eternity (Isa. 47:8; Rev. 18:7) and celebrated their divine achievement of universal rule (Isa. 14:13-14; Dan. 4:30; Rev. 13:5-8). These were certainly narratives of closure justifying oppression and suppressing all dissent. It is against these dominant narratives that the biblical metanarrative takes on its most imperial and militant colors, especially in the visions of Daniel and Revelation, which assert the transcendent power of God over all would-be divine rulers on earth and foresee their destruction and supersession by the rule of God triumphant over all evil. These visions empower nonviolent resistance to oppression, enabling God's people to continue to refute the finality and divinity of the empires. They do not suggest that the kingdom of God is merely a more powerful or more successful version of the imperial powers, but that it is an altogether different kind of rule. The tragic irony of Christian history has been that so often Christian empires have taken over the symbol of the kingdom of God to justify the same kind of rule as those of the empires it was forged to oppose. What has happened in these cases is that the biblical metanarrative has been transformed into a metanarrative much more like those Lyotard rejects, that is, a metanarrative that functions to legitimate existing structures of power.

(7) Not only is the biblical metanarrative a story of God's repeated choice of the dominated and the wretched, the powerless and the marginal. It also breaks the cycle by which the oppressed become oppressors in their turn. This is the effect of the memory of exodus in Israel's laws (e.g., Lev. 19:34). The cross is the event in which the cycle is definitively broken. The christological passage in Philippians 2 means that Jesus' obedience to the point of identification with the human condition at its most wretched and degraded, the death of the slave or the criminal, is what qualifies him to exercise the divine rule from the cosmic throne of God. Only the human

---

19. See Richard Bauckham, *Gospel Women: Studies of the Named Women in the Gospels* (Grand Rapids: Eerdmans; Edinburgh: T&T Clark, 2002), chap. 1.

who has thus identified himself irrevocably with the lowest of the low can be entrusted with the power that God exercises characteristically on their behalf. Distortion of the biblical story into an ideology of oppression has to suppress the biblical meaning of the cross.

(8) While these characteristics of the biblical metanarrative make it a story uniquely unsuited to being an instrument of oppression in the usual senses of that term, postmodernism has invented a new sort of oppression or injustice, consisting in any claim to universal truth, whatever the character of that claim. Disillusioned by the failure of the modern hope of the emancipatory power of reason, postmodernism has decided that, so far from setting free, truth oppresses because it delegitimizes difference.[20] This claim must simply be contested. For a start, there is the relativist paradox: the need to insist that there is one truth — the truth that there is no truth — and one justice — the right of every voice to equal status. The incommensurability of language games should make it impossible to persuade others of the need to respect difference. Agonistic politics becomes nothing more than a power struggle between the competing interests of the heterogeneous groups. By contrast, a perspective that recognizes and claims truth can be genuinely open to dialogue and the truth of the other. Presumably a metanarrative that really claims comprehensive understanding of reality and to have already subsumed all other narratives cannot be open to other truth, but it is fair to ask, with Eagleton, whether such a metanarrative[21] is not now in any case something of an Aunt Sally. The threat of totalitarianism should not be neglected, but the fact that relativism appears to be its polar opposite does not make relativism the most effective safeguard against that threat. To the totalitarianism of twentieth-century regimes the biblical metanarrative has more effectively inspired resistance than anything resembling postmodernism has. But the challenge to the church in the postmodern context is to reclaim the biblical story in a way that expresses its noncoercive claim to truth without imposing eschatological closure.

20. William C. Placher, *Narratives of a Vulnerable God* (Louisville: Westminster John Knox, 1994), pp. 120-21, gives an illuminating example: "In writing about the Spanish invasion of the Americas, Tzvetan Todorov compares Pedro de Alvarado, who murdered native Americans, with Bartolomé de Las Casas who, as a Christian, loved them, opposed violence, and sought to convert them. Todorov finds little enough difference: 'Is there not already a violence in the conviction that one possesses the truth oneself, whereas this is not the case for others?'" (quotation from Tzvetan Todorov, *The Conquest of America,* trans. Richard Howard [New York: Harper & Row, 1987], p. 169).

21. More precisely, teleological history: Eagleton, *The Illusions,* pp. 45, 104-5.

CHAPTER 2

Are We Still Missing the Elephant?
C. S. Lewis's "Fernseed and Elephants"
Half a Century On

Lewis delivered the lecture that was later titled "Fernseed and Elephants" to the Anglican ordinands studying at Westcott House, Cambridge, in 1959. It was originally called "Modern Theology and Biblical Criticism,"[1] but its subject was more specifically the kind of criticism of the Gospels represented by Rudolf Bultmann. His real concern was with what he calls a "theology which denies the historicity of nearly everything in the Gospels to which Christian life and affections and thought have been fastened for nearly two millennia."[2] He was singularly unimpressed by the New Testament scholarship that was widely held to have cast so much doubt on the historical reliability of the Gospels, and he urged his hearers not to reserve their skepticism for the New Testament and the creeds, but to try doubting the critics instead.

It would be fascinating to know how this lecture was received by its original hearers, especially as Lewis made some trenchant points about the difficulties they would find, as clergy, if they were to try to apply such a theology honestly in their ministry. But I do not know any evidence of how it went down. I suspect it had the impact of marmite, and it still has an uncompromising taste that readers are likely either to love or to hate. However, before considering Lewis's arguments, it will be helpful to ask how far the sea of New Testament scholarship has changed since he dipped a dubious toe into it in 1959.

---

1. C. S. Lewis, "Modern Theology and Biblical Criticism," in *Christian Reflections* (London: Bles, 1967), pp. 152-66. My references are to this edition. It was later published under the title "Fernseed and Elephants" in Clive Staples Lewis, *Fern-Seed and Elephants and Other Essays on Christianity* (London: Fontana, 1975).

2. Lewis, "Modern Theology and Biblical Criticism," p. 153.

What Has Changed?

One obvious development is the huge proliferation of research and publications in the subject, which has made it impossible for any one scholar or even group of scholars to wield the authority in the field that Lewis perceived Bultmann to do. With that proliferation has gone an increasing diversity of methods, which an "educated outsider" such as Lewis professed himself to be will likely find bewildering. Nevertheless, there is a sense in which Bultmann and other major names in the subject retain a remarkable authority. I think this is due to the prevailing understanding of New Testament scholarship as a progressive science in which each generation of scholars builds on the results achieved by previous scholarship. Everyone in the field is familiar with a narrative in which the source criticism of the Gospels (often considered the lasting legacy of the nineteenth century) was followed by form criticism (the contribution of Bultmann and Dibelius), which itself was followed by redaction criticism, then literary criticism, and then (finally?) social-scientific criticism. The key feature of this narrative is that each new approach is understood not to undermine the achievements of the previous approaches, but rather to add a further story to the gradually building structure.

Source criticism of the Gospel of John is a good example of the conservatism of the scholarly tradition. When literary scholarship, attending to the literary dynamics of the text as we have it, rather than judging it by the standard of how the modern critic might write such a text, began to show how the final form of the Gospel can be read as a coherent whole, some scholars did see that this undermined the basis for the old sort of source criticism, dependent as it was on the perception of so-called aporias in the text. But others insisted that this new literary appreciation of the text as we have it can only be a new level laid on the top of the earlier levels, without disturbing them.

In my view this understanding of New Testament scholarship as an incremental science is a deeply misleading one, but their education in the discipline strongly disposes many scholars to treat it as axiomatic. While their skepticism is well developed in many respects, it is directed in the directions the scholarly tradition has pointed, not back toward major features of the tradition itself. This is why a broad skepticism about the historical reliability of the Gospels continues to be widely prevalent, and the many important reasons for questioning that skepticism, even when advanced by major scholars such as Martin Hengel, fail to make the degree of impact they should. One major desideratum is the deconstruction of the prevalent narrative of the scholarly tradition, which rests on the privileging of certain scholars and developments, while other scholars who at the same time took other approaches and often made cogent criticisms of such developments have been systematically forgotten. The continuing, exponential increase in publications in the field is a real hindrance in this respect. It is very difficult for anyone to keep up with recent literature in even part of the field, and the temptation to rely on a simplistic narrative of developments in the less recent past is therefore strong. But we must become more aware that students and laypeople are often fed a tendentious account of the subject that makes it seem more similar than it really is to the kind of incremental science whose major results must be simply accepted as given.

This is not to say that there are not lasting achievements on which we can all build, only that we must be more discriminating in our discernment of them, for the dominant scholarly tradition also took some seriously mistaken directions that need to be corrected. Much work that has been pursued in those directions will have to be left aside, however disorientating that may be. In my view, the biggest mistake in Gospels scholarship was form criticism and the criteria of authenticity that the quest of the historical Jesus consequently found it necessary to adopt. Criticisms of form criticism and of the criteria have been mounting, and Gospels scholars really do need to get on in earnest with the debate about what should replace them. How the historical reliability of the Gospels may fare in that debate remains an open question, but we should be clear that the reasons for skepticism that the form critics promoted, which are the reasons why the Gospels have come to be treated as unreliable history in much theological education and in the popular impressions of the subject that are now widely prevalent, are not at all secure.

Their education and their experience of students have made many New Testament scholars especially wary of seeming to give succor to "fundamentalism." They are more disposed to encourage skepticism toward the Gospels than confidence in them. But the frequency with which one now finds "educated outsiders" supposing it is doubtful whether Jesus of Nazareth even existed should make us wonder about such priorities. Whereas Lewis imagined the ordinands he addressed preaching to laypeople who believed much more than they did, today's ordinands will have to speak to laypeople familiar with the most radically skeptical views of Gospel historicity as well as to those who may seek to secure their faith against such skepticism by adopting a "fundamentalist" response. Both deserve to be told that Gospels scholarship comes in many forms, hardly any of which are as skeptical about historicity as the ideas promoted in the media, and that there is a great deal of excellent scholarship that warrants a fundamental trust in the historical picture of Jesus painted in the Gospels.

Other developments since Lewis wrote will become relevant as we consider the specific criticisms he leveled at the Gospels scholarship of his time. They certainly bear rereading even in a context that has changed considerably.

The Gospels Scholar and the Literary Critic

Lewis's first line of attack on the Gospels scholarship he knew ought to be his strongest because it brings into play his own professional expertise as a literary critic. He says that he distrusts New Testament scholars "as critics" because they "lack literary judgment."[3] With reference to the form critics Lewis surely has a valid point. Bultmann and his followers were cloth-eared when it came to the literary qualities and literary logic of the Gospels. With the working assumption that the Synoptic evangelists were little more than compilers of discrete oral traditions, they were intent on dissecting the text by detecting what they considered incoherent sequences of material. By contrast, Lewis would now find much Gospel exegesis that expounds the literary coherence of the texts.

But I am not sure he would be entirely pleased with the current state of literary criticism of the Gospels. For one thing, Lewis wrote before the advent of "theory" in literary studies, whereas the literary turn in Gospels studies that occurred in the late twentieth century was stimulated largely by theory-laden approaches emanating from the university departments of literary studies at that time. But, second, the tools of literary criticism that New Testament scholars have applied to the Gospels frequently derived from the study of literary fiction, especially the modern novel. Consequently, all too often it was assumed that the use of such tools entailed regarding the Gospels as fictional story *rather than* history. Indeed, the extreme postmodern direction in which some enthusiasts for literary study of the Gospels tended encouraged the view that historiography is as much

---

3. Lewis, "Modern Theology and Biblical Criticism," p. 154.

fictional story as the ancient romance or the modern novel is. If one is not inclined to such an extreme, then the distinction between fictional narrative and historiography should certainly not be taken to mean that the former employs narrative techniques and the latter does not. Historians, at least in the ancient world, were storytellers too, but the ideal of best historical practice was to tell the story *of what had happened.*

Lewis's claim for literary judgment of the Gospels was very far from later scholars' tendency to assimilate them to fictional story. Quite the contrary, Lewis wished to claim that as a literary critic he could establish the historicity of the Gospel narratives. One might expect such a claim to proceed by identifying the Gospels as belonging to the ancient genre of biography (as many scholars now recognize), or more precisely as contemporary biographies (i.e., written within living memory of their subject), which would have been expected to be based on good historical information. But Lewis is not concerned with the literary qualities of historiography, ancient or modern. What he finds — for example, in the dialogue of Jesus with the Samaritan woman in John's Gospel — is narrative so realistic that it must be either "reportage," nearly as close to the facts as Boswell's record of Dr. Johnson's conversation, or else fictional narrative that uniquely anticipates "the whole technique of modern, novelistic, realistic narrative."[4] Since the latter is incredible, the former must be true.

This is rather typical of Lewis's argumentative style. He liked to reduce matters to a choice of bluntly stated alternatives, only one of which seems credible. But, in this case, Lewis would seem to be saying that the Gospel of John is neither fictional story *nor historiography,* but a naïve report of what Jesus and the Samaritan woman actually said. From a literary critic of Lewis's stature, this is surely an astonishing claim. How can he have failed to recognize this evangelist's storytelling skills? How can he not have noticed that, along with the elements of "realism" in the Johannine dialogues, there is also an artificiality to them? For example, again and again Jesus' interlocutors misunderstand his figurative statements by taking them in a crassly literal sense. This is a technique by which the evangelist gives Jesus the opportunity to indicate the true meaning of such statements. Recognizing such literary artifice by no means entails that John simply invented Jesus' meetings with people such as Nicodemus and the Samaritan woman, though this is often supposed. It does mean that, if such meetings took place, John has given a skillfully contrived literary *represen-*

4. Lewis, "Modern Theology and Biblical Criticism," p. 155.

tation of them, not something like the contents of a reporter's notebook. This is what one would expect of ancient historiography.

Lewis was reacting against the claim that John's Gospel was "a spiritual romance" or "a poem not history." There is force to his claim that he had been "reading poems, romances, vision-literature, legends, myths all my life,"[5] and that "not one of them" is like John's Gospel. But he strangely fails to reckon with historiography as literature. In my view, first-century people would easily have identified John's Gospel as some kind of historiography. New Testament scholars who judge it to be unreliable history have resorted much too readily to saving its "truth" by supposing it was never meant to be historiography. Lewis is right to that extent. But historiography is literature. Historians, then and now, deploy literary artifice. Moreover, historiography comes in many varieties, which have their own literary conventions, their various different ways of *representing* what happened in the past, since the past cannot be simply *reproduced*. In such a context, there may well be interesting work to be done on the elements of "realism" in Gospel narratives. We may be able to judge some of these likely to derive from personal recollection of the events. Whether such material is more characteristic of the Gospels than of other examples of ancient historiography is also a question well worth pursuing. (It was evidently not one that occurred to Lewis.) But simply to suppose that narratives are historically reliable to the extent that they lack literary artistry is no more convincing in the case of the Gospels than it would be in the case of Lewis's own autobiographical narrative in *Surprised by Joy.*

Another respect in which Lewis finds Bultmann, in particular, lacking in literary judgment concerns the personality of Jesus. According to Bultmann, not only did the New Testament writers attach no importance to the personality of Jesus, but also "the tradition of the earliest Church did not even unconsciously preserve a picture of his personality."[6] I sympathize with Lewis's scorn: "What evidence have we that [Bultmann] would recognize a personality if it were there?"[7] That most readers of the Gospels do feel that "in the Gospels they have met a personality" is surely true, and Gospels scholarship has for various reasons, not only those that were decisive for Bultmann, neglected this issue. I am not sure that the personality of Jesus is as easy to describe as Lewis thinks ("peasant shrewdness,

5. Lewis, "Modern Theology and Biblical Criticism," p. 155.
6. Lewis, "Modern Theology and Biblical Criticism," p. 156.
7. Lewis, "Modern Theology and Biblical Criticism," p. 156.

intolerable severity, and irresistible tenderness").[8] I am highly skeptical of Lewis's claim that there are only three historical figures whom we feel we know as if by personal acquaintance: Plato's Socrates, Boswell's Dr Johnson, and the Jesus of the Gospels. This is the kind of bold assertion that makes Lewis's writing so stimulating, but I doubt it would bear more thorough consideration. What about, for example, Queen Elizabeth I or Augustine of Hippo or even Herod the Great? (I suppose Lewis must be implicitly discounting, as not really "historical," the many nineteenth- and twentieth-century persons whom we can know intimately from diaries, correspondence, and plentiful personal memoirs.) I wonder if Lewis's judgment here doesn't reflect, once again, the fact that he read far more poetry and romance than he did historiography?

Though it raises important questions, I find this part of Lewis's essay, which because it brings his professional judgment as a literary critic into play one would expect to be the strongest part, actually rather disappointing and all too idiosyncratic. I suspect it fails largely because, while Lewis's purpose in the essay is to vindicate the traditional Christian view of the Gospels as history, he was not generally very interested in history. His own expertise and interests were in types of literature very different from historiography. Myths, romances, and epic poetry were his world. In judging the Gospels not to be such, he is on solid ground. But he is oddly uninterested in what sort of literature they actually are.

However, I cannot leave this part of Lewis's essay without commenting on his observation that critics such as Bultmann studied the New Testament texts intensively but lacked a wide and deep experience of literature in general. Of contemporary New Testament scholars one could certainly say that they often acquire considerable expertise in other specific bodies of ancient literature that seem relevant to the study of the New Testament. They are sometimes also expert in scholarly methodologies pursued in other disciplines (the social sciences, literature, etc.). But Lewis might well still complain that these are narrowly professional interests. What he expected of scholars in the humanities was the kind of broad exploration of literature for the love of it and for the sheer human interest of it that he himself pursued from a young age. As more recent literary critics who exemplify this, in very different ways, one thinks of George Steiner and Terry Eagleton.

For scholars in such a tradition it would be inconceivable that one

8. Lewis, "Modern Theology and Biblical Criticism," p. 156.

could have real insight into such texts as the New Testament if one did not have the kind of broad humanistic interests that make people *want,* for the sheer intellectual value of it, to read Plato or Nietzsche, Sophocles or Shakespeare, Rilke or Basho, Virginia Woolf or Tolstoy, Wittgenstein or Buber (and so on without end — I am not meaning to suggest any kind of canon of great writers). But in the professionalized and careerist world of contemporary New Testament studies such interests count for nothing, whereas keeping abreast of every new monograph in the small segment of the discipline one has adopted as one's professional patch is indispensable. Moreover, professional expertise and productivity are supposedly quantifiable, whereas the insight and wisdom that Lewis seeks are not.

Miracles

Lewis has three further criticisms of the Gospels scholarship of his day. Because my space is limited, I shall pass over the second and note the third only briefly. This is that he found in these scholars "a constant use of the principle that the miraculous does not occur." Lewis, in my view rightly, points out that whether the miraculous is possible is "a purely philosophical question. Scholars, as scholars, speak on it with no more authority than anyone else."[9] Since Lewis wrote there have been influential arguments to the effect that historical method as such excludes the possibility of the miraculous, at least from the scope of the historian's work, and many New Testament scholars have accepted this principle as necessary to their attempt to be rigorously historical. But one should also mention Wolfhart Pannenberg's impressive attempt to reformulate historical method in such a way that the historian can affirm the historicity of the resurrection of Jesus. The issue is a complex one, which deserves more theoretical reflection from scholars who axiomatically, as it were, bring a narrowly secular worldview to their study of the texts.

Speculative History

In my view Lewis scores his best points with his fourth line of attack, in which he critiques highly speculative accounts of how the texts came to be

9. Lewis, "Modern Theology and Biblical Criticism," p. 158.

written and how early Christian thought developed in the New Testament period. He gives modern examples from his own experience of how easily modern reviewers can be mistaken about such matters even in the case of work by their own contemporaries, such as Lewis himself. The best known of his examples is the suggestion by many reviewers that the Ring in Tolkien's *The Lord of the Rings* was suggested by the atomic bomb. It seems highly plausible but for the fact that the known chronology of the composition of Tolkien's work makes it impossible.

Since Lewis wrote, the scope for speculative hypotheses about Gospel origins has actually increased. From the 1960s onward many scholars have been busy reconstructing the alleged "community" in which each of the Gospels is supposed to have been written and to which it was addressed. The impression is often given that, while the Gospels offer little reliable evidence about the historical Jesus, they reflect almost transparently the very specific historical circumstances in which they were written. The attempt to reconstruct Gospel communities is the more seductive because it claims to be hermeneutically important, even essential. Many a commentary designed to guide preachers and laypeople invites them to put themselves in the dogmatically described position of a Gospel's small group of original hearers in order to recover its original meaning. Lewis's strictures could still serve to expose the absurd degree of confidence such reconstructions exude. We must dispel the illusion that understanding the Gospels depends on them.

Historical speculation is not necessarily a bad thing. It can stimulate enquiry. The reason it has so often led Gospels scholars astray is that they are not in the habit of distinguishing their more probable conclusions from their more speculative flights of fancy. Moreover, they seem oblivious of the mathematical point that Lewis makes: that as one hypothesis is laid upon another, probability steadily decreases. In my view the misleading conviction that New Testament scholarship is an incremental scientific discipline has a lot to do with this. A widely accepted hypothesis gets to be treated as a firm foundation on which a new hypothesis can be safely erected, when in reality it remains a hypothesis, which no degree of consensus can turn into a fact. Consensus often has as much to do with the sociology of knowledge as it has with the compelling nature of the hypothesis. I remember the angry bafflement of a scholar who could not accept my statement that Q is a hypothesis, even though I said it was quite a probable hypothesis. He insisted that Q is a fact!

Lewis effectively punctured speculative bubbles of Gospels scholarship with personal anecdote and common sense. I would add that Gospels scholars need to learn historical method, not within the claustrophobic confines of the dominant tradition of Gospels scholarship, but amid the broad horizons of ordinary historical scholarship. But, as a starting point, Lewis's essay remains a bracingly provocative attempt to restore some perspective to a discipline that seems peculiarly prone to lose it. All too often it remains the case that, in Lewis's words, those who "claim to see fern-seed . . . can't see an elephant ten yards away in broad daylight."[10]

10. Lewis, "Modern Theology and Biblical Criticism," p. 157.

CHAPTER 3

Contemporary Western Culture — A Biblical-Christian Critique

To characterize the culture of the contemporary West is no easy task. In the late twentieth century it was commonly said that Western society was in transition from a "modern" to a "postmodern" worldview (though some preferred the term "late modern"). But key characteristics of modernity continue to play an important role, especially in the dominant political and economic discourse, alongside the postmodern cultural current that continues to influence both popular and "high" culture. The younger they are, the more the average person's outlook on life can be characterized as postmodern. But it may be that we are witnessing, not a transition from modernity to postmodernity, but an emerging culture that mixes features of each. At any rate, we have currently to reckon with features generally considered modern and features generally considered postmodern, co-existing to varying degrees according to generation and region. With reference to this last factor, for example, the United States remains a more modern culture than Western Europe. In what follows I have selected three themes that seem to me dominant in contemporary Western culture. Naturally, they do not enable an exhaustive account.

Metanarratives

The Metanarrative of Progress

A defining characteristic of modernity, since the European Enlightenment of the late eighteenth century, has been its metanarrative of progress. This was first called a "metanarrative" or "grand narrative" by French postmodernist philosophers, among whom Jean-François Lyotard famously defined the postmodern as "incredulity towards metanarratives."[1] He was thinking primarily of the various versions of Enlightenment progressivism. But the concept of a metanarrative, defined in a somewhat more general sense, provides a useful way of comparing religious or secular worldviews, especially those that provide a framework of meaning for life by telling a story about the world. Broadly Western metanarratives, including those of Marxism, Islam, Christianity, and secular humanism, include some account of where human history is heading.

The overriding idea that has made the modern world is that the extension of knowledge and the application of human reason are able to shape the world and human society in a process of constant improvement of the human condition. History is a great march of human reason toward utopia. Progress is conceived as somehow inevitable, a law of history, though one that requires all the best efforts of human reason to implement it. Progress can be expected to occur in a gradual process of incremental reform, as in liberal democratic versions of the idea, or in a dialectical way, requiring revolution, as in Marxism.

The enormous optimism of modernity derived from its confidence that human reason can master both the natural world and human history, so as to direct history in a progressive direction: toward the greatest human good. The extraordinary achievements of science and technology in the nineteenth century made it the heyday of unqualified faith in progress, but education, bringing enlightenment to the masses, was also a great focus of hope. The progress of reason would make life better in every respect. At the beginning of the twentieth century, intellectuals and politicians confidently expected the abolition of war in the foreseeable future. Against that background, the First World War, which was unprecedented in its cost to human life, was for many deeply disillusioning. The horrors of Nazism and Stalinism dispelled for many the confident expectation that civilization is succeeding barbarism. After all, the Holocaust was not merely atrocious, but a specifically modern sort of atrocity, accomplished with modern technology and modern organizational efficiency. It was also a European act of atrocity, which, along with the exposure of the acts of atrocity committed elsewhere in the world by European powers in the heyday of empires, undermined the previous century's belief that

---

1. Jean-François Lyotard, *The Postmodern Condition,* trans. Geoff Bennington and Brian Massumi (Minneapolis: University of Minnesota Press, 1984), p. xxiv.

Europe was in the vanguard of progress, exporting enlightenment to the rest of the world.

It might seem that such refutations by history should have been mortal blows to the idea of progress, but, so essential is it to the modern West's sense of meaning, it has bounced back. It may be widely admitted that progress is not an entirely inevitable, unilinear process. Setbacks and relapses are possible, but they are still evaluated as such, still measured against progress as the norm. In the politics of the United Kingdom, the words "modernizing" and "progressive" (as opposed to reactionary) are necessary buzzwords even for the elite of the Conservative party. The duty of government is to improve everything. Above all, in the late twentieth century a constantly improving standard of living, funded by economic growth, came to be the confident expectation of people across the whole social spectrum. In a period of unprecedented affluence, the idea of progress, implicit in all economic and political discourse, took especially the form of an expectation of unending economic growth, an expectation that no other society in history has entertained. The financial crisis of 2008 provoked some questioning of the axiom and mechanisms of constant growth, but without major effect.

Although the economic aspect of progress is currently dominant, we should also notice that in Western culture there is a strong sense of moral superiority over the past. It is focused on equality (especially equal rights for women and gay people) and on tolerance of diversity and of people's right to lead their private lives as they choose. Western society is constantly reminding itself that, judged by these standards, it has made huge progress since the 1960s. At the time of the papal election in 2013, the burden of secular comment in the media was that the Catholic Church needs a pope who will "modernize" in these respects.

Postmodern relativism in ethics (see below) does not seem able to dislodge these key symbols of moral progress. Perhaps because they represent success stories for Western societies, they seem to trump what might be regarded as signs of moral decline, such as increasing poverty in Western societies, the decline in charitable giving and volunteering in community service, or the sexualization of children. A major weakness of the idea of progress is that its credibility depends on telling a selective story that favors the beneficiaries of change over the victims. (This is not, of course, a reason for Christians to neglect those moral concerns that contemporary society prioritizes; it merely implies that they should also be alert to moral concerns that contemporary society neglects.)

One recent version of the idea of progress is the neoliberal economic project of globalization, which advocates the unrestricted operation of free-market capitalism and free trade. To its critics this is the latest version of Western imperialism, an ideology that, under cover of a claim to benefit the world, increases the prosperity of the rich at the expense of the poor. Moreover, just as the old imperialism was combined with cultural imperialism (since the superiority of Western culture was axiomatic for the nineteenth-century idea of progress), so economic globalization is accompanied by the Americanization of the world. Dependent for its success on consumerism in both the West and the developing nations, globalization exports the kind of cultural goods that the American dream makes irresistibly attractive to the rest of the world.

Economic globalization, especially in its American version, can also be seen as promoting liberal democracy along with free-market capitalism. The claim is that the two go necessarily together. (Examples as different as Singapore and Russia would seem to contradict this claim.) In this form economic globalization is an idealistic goal, the contemporary version of the myth of America as a messianic nation with a mission to benefit the world. Some of the cultural differences between the United States and Europe are understandable in this light. The loss of their empires by the European powers (including Britain) in the twentieth century was accompanied by a weakening of the notion of European cultural superiority. But in the same period the United States was not losing but gaining an empire, and saw itself as victor in the Cold War, that is, in the ideological battle between conflicting narratives of emancipation (the Marxist and the liberal democratic), in both of which notions of political and economic freedom were closely related. In this light it is not surprising that American culture remains more modern (as opposed to postmodern) than Europe, more wedded to the idea of progress and the values of the Enlightenment (as enshrined in the constitution), more idealistic and optimistic about itself and its role in the world.

Close to the heart of the modern idea of progress was the scientific-technological project of mastering nature and adapting it to human benefit. It was conceived as a kind of liberation of humanity from the constraints of nature. The actual achievements of modern science, not just its vastly increased understanding of the material world but also the fact that this knowledge has been put to so much tangible human advantage, are undoubtedly the major evidence of progress. But such progress has come to seem much more ambivalent in the light of the ecological crisis. Many people in Western societies are more aware that the unintended and un-foreseen consequences of reaching for mastery of nature can turn out to be disastrous, while it no longer seems so obvious that there is a single, indisputably beneficial direction for technological advance to take. None-theless, science retains great prestige.

The obvious success of science leads some to the view that science is the only sort of real knowledge. In the so-called new atheism the scien-tific understanding of the world is represented as superseding a religious worldview. Religious beliefs are merely primitive ways of attempting to explain what science now explains in a properly rational way. The progress of reason should therefore lead to the obsolescence of religion. If religion has actually been making a comeback, as some observers claim, ardent secularists are all the more anxious to oppose it in the name of progress.

The Postmodernist Critique of the Modern Metanarratives

For modernity the metanarrative of progress is a way of salvation, the route to solving the problems of human life. For postmodernists (and for the time being I refer to intellectual people who deliberately adopt a postmodern approach) metanarratives are the problem. We need to be liberated from them, because all such grand projections of universal truth and meaning are oppressive. This charge has two aspects. The first is that a metanarra-tive is a deceptive ideology, disguising military domination or economic exploitation with the claim to be in the vanguard of history, advancing the cause of humanity at large. Such a critique can be devastating to ideologies of empire and globalization.

However, the second way in which metanarratives are considered oppressive is more far-reaching. It holds that all claims to universal truth are necessarily oppressive, because they amount to imposing someone's truth on others. To live within a metanarrative is to be given certain goals and values as though they were the only valid ones. We have to be liberated from metanarratives in order to choose our own goals and values for our-selves. We must and can make our own meanings, without regarding them as uniquely valid. As Andrew Lloyd-Webber's song puts it, "Any dream will do."

This form of relativism has permeated Western culture. It takes pop-ular form in such common expressions as "Everyone has the right to their own opinion" and in the frequently expressed dislike of religion because it tells people what they must believe and what they should do. Actually most people who readily express such views also endorse at least some of the certainties of Enlightenment progress. They would probably not support the teaching of creationism in schools as a valid alternative to Darwinism. They would almost certainly not support the right of pedophiles to pursue their preferred sexual practices. In a society subject to a variety of cultural influences such inconsistency is not surprising.

Another relevant aspect of postmodernity is that it gives primacy to the present. The metanarrative of progress privileges the future: the best is still to come. Postmodern disillusion with the grand political projects and utopias of modernity stresses instead the enjoyment of the present for its own sake. Life does not have to be seen as a journey or a task. It can be a series of liberating moments of euphoric experience. For some observers of culture, however, this cultural moment is already passing, succeeded by a foreboding sense of the demands of the future. In insecure times, the individual detached from the corporate goals and values of modernity may nevertheless become a new kind of responsible individual: the person who keeps fit, lives healthily, lives with a degree of self-imposed discipline, stays flexible to fit into a transient and changing job market, thinks about their pension. This too can be a postmodern choice — or perhaps a "hyper-modern" one.[2]

The Biblical-Christian Metanarrative in Post/modernity

The modern idea of progress undoubtedly has its roots in the Christian tradition, which first taught Western society to envisage history as a meaningful process orientated to the future. What transformed the Christian view into the modern idea of progress was the loss of divine transcendence and the substitution of human mastery over nature and history. The future goal of history was now down to human reason and human power, working solely with the immanent potential of this world. In an important sense humans assumed what, in the Christian tradition, had been the role of God. The Promethean character of the idea of progress, in its more utopian political or more visionary-scientific forms, is the obvious consequence of this assumption of divinity. But Christians were frequently able to assimilate the biblical metanarrative to the modern idea of progress, envisaging

2. See Gilles Lipovetsky, *Hypermodern Times,* trans. Andrew Brown (Cambridge: Polity, 2005).

the working of God through human agency and identifying the goals of progress with the coming of the kingdom of God. The idea of progress remains, indeed, a core assumption of many Christians.

In a situation where the idea of progress has proved remarkably durable but also problematic, some hard questions need to be asked. Is the idea of progress an appropriate modern form for the biblical metanarrative to take in our time, or do we need to recover the distinctives of the biblical metanarrative? Is the biblical metanarrative itself vulnerable to the postmodern critique? Or does it present a credible alternative to both the modern metanarrative and the postmodern rejection of metanarratives?

As a preliminary response to these questions, I shall briefly indicate some features of the biblical metanarrative:[3]

(1) What perhaps most distinguishes the biblical metanarrative from all versions of the modern one is that it is not a narrative of human mastery. What accounts for history in the biblical view is neither human mastery nor meaningless randomness but the freedom and purpose of God and the freedom of humans to obey or to resist God and his purpose. The "plot" of history is the purpose of God within which there is space also for human freedom. So human achievement is celebrated where it should be and human evil condemned where it should be, but history cannot be mastered and directed by humans. Since history is often manifestly what turns out rather than what humans intend, this seems a more reasonable understanding of history that nevertheless does not abandon history to meaninglessness, but sets hope for ultimate meaning on God.

(2) History is not rationally explicable and calculable in the way that the modern project of mastering and directing it requires. God's purpose is revealed, but his workings are often mysterious. In particular, the biblical metanarrative does not explain evil, as though it were a problem reason can solve and surmount. God is at work where humans resist evil, but the biblical metanarrative engages evil not with explanation but with hope for God's redemption from and incalculable overcoming of evil.

(3) The transhistorical dimension is essential to the biblical metanarrative. In other words, its hope is that God will bring his whole creation to fulfillment in a new creative act that takes it far beyond the potentialities inherent in this world alone. God works within history for the sake of his kingdom that transcends history. This does not render human activity for good in this world pointless, because all that is good in this world will be

3. For a fuller discussion see chap. 1 above.

taken up by God into his new creation. On the other hand, it avoids the progressivist tendency to value activity for good only if it adds to an incremental process of progressive improvement. Even the most transient good is worth achieving for its own sake, and in the new creation it will not be lost.

(4) Limited to the immanent possibilities of history, the idea of progress can offer hope and a kind of salvation only to the beneficiaries of progress. It offers no hope for the victims of history, the countless numbers whose lives have been short and largely miserable, or for the victims of progress itself (for modern achievements always benefit some at the expense of others). The biblical metanarrative opens a future for the dead, when God "will wipe away every tear from every eye" (Rev. 21:4).

(5) The gospel at the heart of the biblical metanarrative invites without compelling. This belongs to the very nature of the gospel and is compromised whenever the church aligns itself too closely with coercive power. That it is more than just someone's truth imposed on others becomes apparent only as the true nature of God becomes apparent to people in a form of conviction that is more than narrowly rational. It is neither the universal truth of the Enlightenment, evident to any rational person, nor a purely subjective truth "that works for me" but actually lacks transformative power. The biblical metanarrative requires the church's mission to convey *this kind* of truth.

(6) The relationship of the particular to the universal in the biblical metanarrative is important. Again and again the focus is on the particular — Israel, Jesus, specific communities of early Christians — but in such a way as to claim universal relevance for these historical particulars. God's purpose moves always from the particular to the universal, and taking seriously the particularity of every human context into which the gospel comes. It values the particular in a way that the abstract universality of Enlightenment rationalism does not, but it gives the particular more than the purely local meaning that is all that is available in the postmodern shift to the particular. It is important for the church's mission to embody the biblical way of relating the universal and the particular.

(7) The biblical metanarrative offers a framework for meaningful living in both the individual and the social dimensions. The Bible has many small-scale stories of the kind that would not appear in history written as a grand narrative of advancing progress. But the individual does not have to invent a private meaning of their own. In relationship with the God who values both the individual and the world, individuals and groups can

participate in a meaning that opens up their own lives to the wider context of God's purpose for his whole creation.

Freedom and Individualism

In the contemporary West freedom is a hugely potent and alluring word. It is the primary value of modernity and postmodernity alike. But it is a "big" word, with a wide and flexible range of meaning, and any attempt to analyze and engage with contemporary culture needs to reflect seriously on what it has come to mean today.

It was the Enlightenment that first gave freedom the primacy it has come to enjoy, and there is an aspect of the Enlightenment's legacy that almost all contemporary people would agree is valuable: its insistence on the rights of the individual over against the power of society or the state. Ideas of the dignity of the individual and the fundamental human rights of the individual, which must be universally respected, took their modern form through the Enlightenment, though they have roots in the Christian tradition. Some people now associate talk of human rights with hyper-individualism and the decline of social obligation — rights without responsibilities — but this is the fault, not of the idea of human rights itself, but of the decay of a wider context of values.

However, modern concepts of freedom range much more widely than those that are enshrined in democratic political systems. In the spirit of modernity there is an aspiration to freedom from all limits whatever. The notion that humanity can break free of nature by transcending any limits was an influential factor in the modern scientific-technological project of domination of nature. The ecological crisis has reminded those who attend to it that there simply are limits in the nature of things that cannot be disregarded with impunity. In other words human beings are finite creatures.

The understanding of freedom as an ability, even a right to break out of all restrictions, has been very damaging also when adopted as an idea of individual freedom. Modern individuals came to think that the more freedom they have the better and that the freedom they wanted was self-determination. For this understanding of freedom other people can only be restrictions on my freedom. Society becomes a sort of contract in which independent individuals promise not to exercise our own freedom to the extent of impinging on other people's freedom. This makes freedom and community seem incompatible. Obligations to other people restrict freedom. Accordingly, the lowest-common-denominator morality of contemporary Western culture puts obligation to others in an entirely negative form: Do what you like so long as you don't harm anyone else. This is what we are left with if freedom for the individual is understood as transcending all limits and if freedom is detached from a context of other values, as has tended to happen in the contemporary West.

Freedom as Maximal Independence

Modern individualistic freedom is in full-scale revolt against the given. This means not only that it regards given limits as unwelcome restrictions but also that freedom is conceived as complete independence. That is, it rejects dependence. Freedom is not received from others or enhanced by others. Freedom is an inherent capacity that the individual deploys in an exercise of self-creation. Each has the freedom to choose who they will be.

This kind of freedom as maximal independence makes people unwilling to make long-term commitments or to stick with relationships or situations that are not going well. People want the right to move on. They want to keep their options open. They hate being dependent on others. All these facets of freedom are antithetical to community, which requires such old-fashioned virtues as faithfulness and commitment. Or, to put it another way: maximal independence is incompatible with belonging. Of course, people still want to belong, but they often experience the desire to belong as in considerable tension with freedom. They get divorced and then they regret it. Or they want lifelong loving commitment to a partner, but feel it would be unbearably restrictive actually to marry. Family relationships are obvious victims of freedom as maximal independence, but neighborliness is another.

Freedom as Consumer Choice

Alongside freedom as maximal independence, the other dominant aspect of freedom in contemporary Western culture is the freedom of consumer choice. Having choice can certainly be a good thing, but we may well wonder whether our society has not gone about as far as it can in multiplying choice in every aspect of life that can be bought. Consumer choice can be a means of commercial manipulation cloaking itself in the illusion of freedom. But probably the worst manifestation of a consumer culture occurs when the model of consumer choice is applied to things other than those we purchase, such as choosing our moral values.

The effect of a culture that overvalues consumer choice is to give the impression that freedom is really enhanced by the mere multiplication of choices, regardless of how we exercise choice. What matters is having the choice, not making the right choice, not choosing well or rightly. This is one of the points where one may fear that freedom is becoming the only value. Distinguishing good choices and bad choices is serious when there are accepted notions of good and bad. In a culture that socializes people into a range of values and virtues that constitute the good life, the main value of choice will be that it enables the making of good choices. Freedom is a faculty and choice an opportunity *for the good*. But without a widely accepted range of values and virtues, choice becomes the good that is valued in and of itself.

Freedom and Consumer Choice

Usually regarded as a postmodern development of freedom is the notion that truth is a matter of wholly subjective choice. If this really does mean that any choice of values is equally valid, then it makes freedom the only necessary and common value. Few people really go to such an extreme. But relativism gains what strength it has from the value placed on freedom as mere individual choice as well as from the pluralism of contemporary Western society. Where a wide variety of cultural and religious traditions coexist, it seems difficult to respect difference without treating the differences as matters of indifference. The real problem lies not in the pluralism itself, for it is in such particular traditions that values are fostered and people learn to practice them. The problem is that an increasingly secular society encourages people to stand outside any such tradition. When the supposedly self-evident universal values of the Enlightenment come to be seen, in postmodernity, as themselves just one tradition, then freedom is in danger of becoming the value that always trumps others.

A Biblical-Christian Understanding of Freedom

In the contemporary context it is vital that Christians develop a positive understanding of freedom that provides a real alternative to the highly problematic dominant one. Some key ingredients would be:

(1) The Bible does value freedom *from* oppressive conditions or forces of all kinds. God delivered Israel from slavery in Egypt. Jesus delivered people from demonic oppression, crippling physical impairments, and social isolation. But the New Testament is also notable for its profound diagnosis of humans as in bondage to sin (e.g., John 8:34; Rom. 6:6). Liberation from external constraints is not enough. There are compulsions and addictions to evil from which one must be freed.

(2) Freedom is finite. It has to be exercised within given limits. Independence is possible only in dependence on God and within the complex web of interdependence that is human society. Both for the sake of community and for the sake of the ecological health of the planet, recovering a notion of limits is vital.

(3) Freedom is not merely *from*, but also *for*. It is for the living of the good life for which humans are created. In particular, freedom is fulfilled in service to God and to others. It is significant that the Bible's understanding of freedom requires this paradox (e.g., 1 Pet. 2:16; Rom. 6:16-19). Unlike the compulsion to sin from which believers are freed by Christ, the service for which they are freed is the willing commitment of love. Indeed, freedom is properly conceived and exercised only in relationship to love, love that both grants freedom and makes service an expression of freedom. True freedom thrives, not in isolation, as independence of others and as choice of values for oneself, but in reciprocity with others (God, other humans, and other creatures) and within a framework of normative values.[4]

Consumerism and Excess

Over the last half century Western societies have achieved a degree of affluence that is wholly unparalleled in history. Not everyone has benefited: in Britain and the United States the gap between the poorest and the wealthiest is actually increasing. But most people enjoy a material "standard of living" of which their forebears, even in the early twentieth century, never dreamed. Few would deny that some real benefits have accompanied this. But it has also been accompanied by a consumerist culture in which buying and consuming what can be bought (and this can include experiences as well as things) dominate much of life. This is more than old-fashioned greed. Consumerism is an ideology promoted by commercial interests in

4. For further discussion see chap. 5 below.

such a way that it permeates the cultural context that forms people's desires and values. The commercial model of buying and selling objects extends to every area of life that can conceivably be packaged, marketed, and sold for profit. We have already noted the progressivist expectation of constant economic growth and the understanding of freedom as consumer choice. These are vital supports for an economic system that depends on constantly creating new "wants" and frequently turning them into "needs" for what has never before been considered necessary. The presupposition is that human needs for what can be bought are unlimited and human desires for what can be bought are insatiable.[5]

A sign of the cultural power of consumerism is the way it inclines people to identify themselves and to evaluate each other by the standards of purchase and consumption. In its cruder forms this was "keeping up with the Joneses" in accumulation of possessions and in conspicuous consumption. But the rising tide of affluence means that, just as manufacturers need to find new ways of differentiating their products from those of their competitors, so consumers need subtler ways of differentiating themselves as consumers from their neighbors. This is how value comes to attach to such things as designer labels. According to some observers consumerism has entered a phase where style is dominant. We are not just as *wealthy* as our possessions and lifestyle proclaim; we are the *sort of people* our possessions and consumer lifestyle choices indicate. What does your car say *about you?* The maximization of consumer choice makes it possible for consumers to create identities for themselves in more and more varied and subtle ways. But are they expressing who they really are in these consumerist ways, or are these merely postmodern masks behind which people have lost any more substantial identity?

There are many signs that Western society is suffering a damaging addiction to excess. We can no longer distinguish "enough" from excess. Instead of appreciators of the goods of the earth, we have become ever discontented and dissatisfied cravers for more. Yet psychological studies have shown that, although people's level of income does increase their sense of well-being up to a point, beyond that point it makes no difference at all. The significance of such "happiness studies" must be treated with

---

5. For Christian critiques of consumerism, see John Kavanaugh, *Following Christ in a Consumer Society,* new ed. (Maryknoll, N.Y.: Orbis, 2006); Craig Bartholomew and Thorsten Moritz, eds., *Christ and Consumerism: A Critical Analysis of the Spirit of the Age* (Carlisle: Paternoster, 2000).

caution. Happiness can refer to everything from shallow hedonism to the conviction that a considerable sacrifice is worth making because it is the right thing to do. A Christian view of the good life cannot take for granted that happiness, however understood, is the goal of life. But whatever we think about happiness, the evidence of serious damage caused by the pursuit of excess is worrying. Depression, chronic anxiety, and other kinds of mental ills, often caused by excessive stress, have greatly increased, as has obesity. For many people, coping with the recent economic downturn has been much more difficult than it need be because both their way of life and their goals in life depend on a level of affluence that, by any standards other than those of the contemporary West, is very high. If the downturn continues, Western society's inability to distinguish needs from wants and its neglect of goods that cannot be bought will need urgent revision. Of course, this is not to deny that there is genuine hardship among those on very low incomes, but our society's addiction to excess impedes the kind of sharing of resources that is needed to protect the vulnerable.

A Biblical-Christian Critique

The biblical category for such an addiction to excess is idolatry. It fits well into the key characteristics of idolatry:

(1) Idolatry is treating something relative as though it were absolute. This is the biblical critique of, for example, nature religion that deifies aspects of nature or its processes. These aspects of nature are in themselves good, but they are part of God's good creation. To treat them as God, as though they had ultimate value, is to mistake their real nature, to distort them, and to distort one's relationship to them. Creatures cannot bear the weight that is put on them by treating them as divine, and humans are degraded by giving to creatures the worship and service that belong only to God. Idolatry, we could say, is misplaced transcendence. In the case of consumerism, then, the material goods may often be just that, material *goods,* but when buying and consuming them become overriding values, unconstrained by other kinds of good, not subordinated to any higher aims or values, then they become idols, and human life that treats them in that way is debased.

(2) Consumerism can also be seen to be idolatry in the way that human desires for what can be bought are treated as unlimited and have to be treated as unlimited. In the ordinary way of things human desires for

what money can buy can be relatively quickly satiated. We do not really want to overeat to the point of getting ill. We can't watch more than one television program at the same time. But there is also human desire for more than such things that money can buy. In the ordinary way of things this human desire for unlimited good comes to the end of what money can buy, and realizes that it cannot be satisfied by such things. This is the human desire for nothing less than God. What consumerism does is this: by offering endlessly new objects of consumption, it postpones indefinitely the realization that human life is oriented to more than such things; it harnesses the desire for God to material objects of consumption so that, satisfied by none of these, it goes on seeking its goal in object after object offered it by advertising. The insatiability of the desire for God is distracted into insatiability for the products of the market. To realize that true human fulfillment is not going to be found in anything of that kind at all can take very much longer in a consumerist society than in others because there are always plenty of things and experiences one hasn't yet bought, and because such things and experiences are marketed with promises much greater than they can fulfill. It can take a long time to realize the misplacement in misplaced transcendence, and by then we may have given up hoping.

(3) Idolatry, in the biblical portrayal, is enslaving. Because the object of worship and service is not the true God, in whose worship and service true human fulfillment is to be found, but an object unworthy of such worship and service, the result is compulsions and addictions that spoil human life rather than enhancing it. In consumerism the drive to possess and to consume *dominates* lives. The compulsion to work long hours at the expense of all kinds of other human goods is one example. People are food junkies, fashion addicts, chocoholics, captive to computer games or television, not to mention drugs and alcohol, not to mention addiction to shopping as such. Some forms of consumerism make us addicted to immediate gratification — in the words of the advertisement for a credit card: taking the waiting out of wanting — but thereby also incur debts that must be paid later. Other forms of consumerism hold us captive to future goals that must be purchased — a bigger house, a good pension, that extravagant holiday — such that the present must be sacrificed for them. One analysis distinguishes between present-oriented consumers and future-oriented consumers as two cultural types, complementary parts of the consumer economy. Future-oriented consumers lend to present-oriented consumers; present-oriented consumers borrow from future-oriented consum-

ers. Future-oriented consumers overwork in early life and often burn out. Present-oriented consumers have chaotic economic lives.[6]

(4) Idolatry, in the biblical portrayal, is deceitful. Its gods are not truly gods, and so they cannot really deliver what they promise their worshipers. In consumerism, advertising functions as the priesthood of the idols. Advertising — not to pull any punches — regularly lies. Advertisements have long ceased to give information about the products. Their function is to associate the products with all manner of desirable goals well beyond the power of the product to deliver: confidence, innocence, relaxation, love, security, power, naturalness, fun, status, comfort, peace, happy families, romantic love, friendship, excitement, freedom from stress, sex appeal, personal attraction, health, youth, happiness, serenity.[7] To regard all this with postmodern irony is not convincing. Granted the messages, once we spell them out, are often transparently silly: drink this brand of coffee and you will have exciting relationships. No one could really believe that. So it doesn't count as legally misleading. But advertising works, or it wouldn't continue to increase in volume. We enjoy the advertisements, and they do their subtle work of getting around our sense and judgment. We all know the advertisements are often better than the programs — a very revealing observation. It is also suggestive that many television advertisements now resemble dreams. Watching them we collude in the process that spins dreams around the products and leads us into illusion.

Thus consumerism fits very well the main features of idolatry. Idolatry is a biblical-theological concept, not one that is available to a secular worldview. It serves to focus for us aspects of the reality of consumerism that cannot be seen so easily from secular perspectives. Is there also a biblical-theological alternative to the values of consumerism? I suggest four features:

(1) The Bible encourages us to seek human fulfillment primarily in loving relationships — that is, relationships not mediated by money or profit — with other people, with the rest of creation, and with God. The jubilee legislation is a signal example of the way the Torah puts community before profit. Jesus, even more radically, promotes an economy of gift and sharing, rooted in the recognition that all good comes from the generous God.

---

6. See Alan Storkey, "Post-Modernism Is Consumption," in *Christ and Consumerism: A Critifcal Analysis of the Spirit of the Age,* ed. Craig Bartholomew and Thorsten Moritz (Carlisle: Paternoster, 2000), pp. 110-17, here pp. 110-11.

7. Storkey, "Post-Modernism Is Consumption,"pp. 113-14.

(2) The Bible insistently views economic affairs from the perspective of the poor, that is, the truly destitute, those excluded from whatever prosperity is enjoyed by others, those who pay the price and have to be forgotten in the official accountings of profit and loss. This is not a bias in a pejorative sense, but a necessary form that concern for the good of all has to take. The acid test of whether an economic system is truly for the benefit of all is whether it benefits the poorest. This is a much more demanding test than whether people in general and on average are better off.

(3) The Bible works with a concept that was once normal but has been banished from our minds by the ideology of growth and consumerism: the concept of sufficiency. The modern expectation of ever-increasing standards of living, to which every contemporary government is committed as though there were no alternative, is precisely a modern expectation. We no longer have any way of distinguishing between sufficiency and excess. In biblical times, however, as in all societies before modernity, the distinction between sufficiency and excess was pivotal. The poor were those who did not have sufficient, which of course was undesirable. To escape poverty was a legitimate aspiration. But to accumulate wealth, as the rich did, was something quite different and generally disapproved as greed and excess. The extent to which people regarded sufficiency as normal and even ideal can be seen from the Old Testament's classic picture of utopian existence, frequently repeated in prophetic visions of the future: "everyone under their vine and their fig tree" (e.g., Mic. 4:4). This is simply the life of the ordinary peasant farmer at its best: owning their own modest smallholding, producing enough to live, and with leisure enough to enjoy it, with no threat from the rapacious rich or foreign invasion. Even in their dreams, Israelite peasants — biblical everyman and everywoman — wanted no more than this in material terms.

We can acknowledge that in this respect much has irrevocably changed, and much has changed genuinely for human good, but can still allow this biblical vision to challenge the unchallengeable in contemporary economics and culture: the dogma of ever-increasing economic growth. The imperative for recovering a concept of sufficiency is now ecological. The *world's resources* are not sufficient for spreading to all the same degree of indulgent excess as Western society has so far reached, let alone continuing in the same direction. From now on, continuing excess for the already affluent can only mean continuing poverty for others.

(4) If consumerism belongs to the category of idolatry in the sense of misplaced transcendence, we need to recognize that the avoidance of idolatry entails the recovery of a true sense of transcendence. Without God, the gap left by the demise of one idolatry will only filled by another, perhaps an even more damaging and dehumanizing one.

CHAPTER 4

The Bible and Globalization

It is debated whether globalization is a new phenomenon of the late twentieth century or goes much further back in history. Of course, this depends on definitions and on which aspects of contemporary globalization are stressed. But it may well be doubted whether the term can usefully be applied to anything in the biblical world of two millennia and more ago. Of course, people in that biblical world had no idea how much larger the inhabited world was than the world they knew. But they already thought globally about the world as far as it was known to extend. Moreover, they spoke about God and the world he created and will redeem in terms that contain, in principle, the whole of this world, whatever the extent of that may actually be found to be. It makes sense to speak of the Bible's global perspective, and the attempt to enter and to understand that perspective may prove relevant to our contemporary context too.

The Supra-global God

The Bible has a global[1] perspective because its God is supra-global, God over all the world. As transcendent beyond the world, this God can be the one source of all things and the goal in which the world will find its unity in the end. This God is the world's Creator, Sustainer, Ruler, Carer, Lover, Savior, and Judge. Not that God is concerned only with generalities; he

---

1. To my use of this word it might be objected that the Bible's usual cosmological picture envisages a flat earth, but I take it "global" no longer means "spherical" but "encompassing the whole world."

observes the death of a sparrow. He works his global purpose through and for the sake of all his particular creatures, human and others. Nor does his transcendence mean remoteness from the world; in Jesus, the incarnate Son of God, God goes to the lengths of solidarity with all his human creatures, and in the Spirit God is deeply and pervasively present throughout his creation. Truly to know this God is inconsistent with every kind of narrow self-interested parochialism or nationalism; rather it lifts the worshiper of God out of a perspective centered on self or a restricted group and into an orientation in love toward all that God loves. Finally, and rather crucially for our purposes, this God is the unique God who tolerates no rivals. Every human attempt to elevate something within the world to godlike status is destructive because the world has been made to find its unifying focus only in the God who made it.

The Bible's perspective is global because it is God-centered. One way to enter this perspective at the right point is to echo some of the language of the Psalms:

> For you, O LORD, are most high over all the earth;
> you are exalted far above all gods. (Ps. 97:9)

> God is king over the nations;
> God sits on his holy throne. (Ps. 47:8)

> The LORD is good to all,
> and his compassion is over all he has made. (Ps. 145:9)

> He will judge the world with righteousness,
> and the peoples with his truth. (Ps. 96:13)

> Make a joyful noise to the LORD, all the earth;
> break forth into joyous song and sing praises. (Ps. 98:4)

Racial Unity and Cultural Diversity (Genesis 10)

For a biblical presentation of global humanity, we must go to the "primeval history" of Genesis 1–11, which serves, within the biblical canon, to sketch the nature of the world within which the rest of the biblical narrative takes place. After the flood, there is something like a new beginning for creation.

In God's covenant with Noah's family and with all other living creatures, God declares his commitment to his creation and sets terms for them to live within it (Gen. 9:1-17). Already we see that the whole of the biblical history that follows has a universal context and relevance, even if this universal horizon may often recede from view behind the more immediate subject matter.

The "global" scene is set more concretely in chapter 10, a "genealogical map of the world"[2] as the world was known to ancient Israel. Here are all the peoples of the known world, all descended from Noah. From our perspective it is a limited world, but from ancient Israel's perspective it pushes the boundaries of the human race. It stretches from Spain in the west (Tarshish) to Iran in the east (Elam), from the Russian steppes in the north (Ashkenaz) to Ethiopia in the south (Cush). Within those limits it gives a remarkably detailed and comprehensive catalog of peoples and places. While many of them are familiar from the histories and prophecies of the Old Testament, some occur only rarely or never outside this catalog, and some are unidentifiable to modern scholars. Nations are included in this inventory not merely for the sake of their historical relationships with Israel but also in a serious and knowledgeable attempt to represent the diversity of nations and places that compose the whole human world. It is a world so far oblivious of Israel, so much so that Canaan is allotted to the Canaanites without comment (10:19). But it is the human world as God's creation, the result of the Creator's intention that humans should fill the earth (Gen. 1:28; 9:7).

While the world of Genesis 10 is concretely limited by the geographical horizon of Israel at some particular historical period, there is also a sense in which it is designed to transcend that limitation. The number of descendants of Shem, Ham, and Japheth listed is precisely seventy.[3] This is a significant number. It must be related to the more common symbolism of the number seven in the Bible, and probably suggests completeness. The number seven in the Bible regularly indicates completeness, but it can also designate a limited number that is intended to stand, representatively, for all. Similarly, we could see the seventy nations of Genesis 10 as

2. Franz Delitzsch quoted by Claus Westermann, *Genesis 1–11,* trans. John J. Scullion (London: SPCK, 1984), p. 528.

3. See also Deut. 32:8, which may mean that there are seventy nations corresponding to the number of the children of Jacob according to Gen. 46:27; Exod. 1:5. See also Luke 10:1, where the seventy (or, in some manuscripts, seventy-two) sent out by Jesus may prefigure the Christian mission to all nations.

a representative list, its seventy quite specific actual nations standing for all nations on earth. It would, of course, be absurd to expect Genesis to name nations or places utterly unknown in Israel's world — Japan or New Zealand or even Britain — but the universal horizon projected by Genesis 10 and the rest of the canonical writings that presuppose it encompasses representatively all other inhabited parts of the world.

When Paul told the Athenian intellectuals that "from one [ancestor]" God "made all nations to inhabit the whole earth" (Acts 17:26), he certainly had Genesis 10 in mind. This chapter, with its derivation of every people from one of the three sons of Noah, clearly presents the human race as what we would now call a single species and the nations as having a fundamental natural kinship with each other. There is no reference to biological differences between them.

On the other hand, there is considerable emphasis on what we would call cultural diversity. The chapter has a refrain, repeated after the list of descendants of each of the sons of Noah and then, with reference to the whole genealogy, at the end:

> These are the descendants of Japheth[4] in their lands, with their own languages,[5] by their families, in their nations. (10:5b)

> These are the descendants of Ham, by their families, their languages, their lands, and their nations. (10:20)

> These are the descendants of Shem, by their families, their languages, their lands, and their nations. (10:31)

> These are the families of Noah's sons, according to their genealogies, in their nations, and from these the nations spread abroad on the earth after the flood. (10:32)

Each nation has its own land, its own language, and its own intergenerational continuity (families or clans). Together these determine what we would call its distinct cultural identity.

---

4. NRSV supplies this phrase (not in the Hebrew), conforming the formula to vv. 20 and 31. Some translations do not, connecting the rest of this sentence with v. 5a, so that it refers only to the descendants of Javan (v. 4).

5. The singular here in NRSV is misleading.

Moreover, Ellen van Wolde, picking up detailed features of the way the nations and their lands are depicted, finds a sociocultural classification in the division of humanity into the descendants of the three sons of Noah:

> The descendants of Japheth are the inhabitants of the coastal regions and the islands. . . . These are population groups which not only live in the west but also belong to the seafaring nations. Whereas in the case of the descendants of Japheth above all the inhabitants of the islands or the coast are named, with Ham we have the great cultivated lands from Egypt to Mesopotamia. This is also why Nimrod is described at such length: he is presented as the founder of a kingdom. He builds . . . the great cities of the then known world. . . . The other descendants of Ham, like Egypt and Canaan, are also sedentary groups which live in a vast area, in villages or cities. . . . The descendants of Shem similarly appear in another light. . . . No cities or villages are mentioned in connection with the descendants of Shem, but only nomadic settlements or tents. . . . As well as being a geographical and ethnographical division, Gen. 10 is thus a sociographic description of the social groups:

> Shem   *is the father of all the children of Eber: the nomads.*
> Ham   *is the father of all the inhabitants of kingdoms and cities: those who are sedentary.*
> Japheth *is the father of all the dwellers of the coasts and islands: the seafarers.*[6]

The more carefully we study it, the more sophisticated this catalog of the nations appears. What van Wolde's examination displays is the economic distinction between peoples who are primarily seafarers or agrarian farmers or nomads, along with the fact that these different economic bases account for a variety of forms of social life.

Genesis 10's refrain with its four elements of nations, lands, languages, and clans is significantly echoed elsewhere in Scripture, though not in precisely this form. Two occurrences in the book of Daniel are instructive for the way the biblical narrative works with a global horizon. In Daniel 4:1, King Nebuchadnezzar addresses "all peoples, nations, and languages that live throughout the earth." This is a conventionally hyper-

---

6. Ellen van Wolde, *Stories of the Beginning: Genesis 1–11 and Other Creation Stories,* trans. John Bowden (London: SCM, 1996), pp. 159-160.

bolic reference to all his subjects,[7] since, although the Babylonian empire came far short of encompassing even the whole of the world known to the peoples of the Middle East at that time, it was the largest that had existed up to that time and is treated in Daniel as the first of the succession of world empires that dominated the Middle East from the sixth century B.C.E. onward. From Nebuchadnezzar down to the Roman emperors and beyond, the rulers of such empires typically claimed the whole world as theirs. (Similarly, it used to be said of the British Empire that the sun never set on it.) But in Daniel 7:13-14, when the figure like a human being ("one like a son of man") comes to the judgment seat of God, there is given to him "dominion and glory and kingship, that all peoples, nations, and languages should serve him." This is God's global kingdom removed from the nations to be given to the figure the New Testament identifies as Jesus Christ.

The book of Revelation also imitates the fourfold formula of Genesis 10, and uses it seven times, varying the terms and their order (as Genesis 10 itself does) such that no one occurrence is the same as any of the others:

> every tribe[8] and language and people and nation (Rev. 5:9)
> all nations and tribes and peoples and languages (Rev. 7:9)
> many peoples and nations and languages and kings (Rev. 10:11)
> peoples and tribes and languages and nations (Rev. 11:9)
> every tribe and people and language and nation (Rev. 13:7)
> every nation and tribe and language and people (Rev. 14:6)
> peoples and multitudes and nations and languages (Rev. 17:15)

This is an instance of the many types of universalistic language used in Revelation. The universality is enhanced by the repetition of the fourfold phrase (four is the number of the earth, with its four directions and four corners) seven times (seven is the number of completeness). The formula is used both of the church, the people of God redeemed from all nations (5:9; 7:9), and of the inhabitants of the world to whom the gospel is proclaimed (14:6), over whom the beast rules (13:7), and whom Babylon the harlot exploits (17:15). The global perspective of the primeval history (Genesis 10), following creation, returns in Revelation as the global perspective of the end-time history, prior to new creation.

---

7. See also Dan. 3:4, 7, 29; 5:19.
8. "tribe" is equivalent to "family" in Genesis 10.

The fourfold formula may indicate an awareness, on the part of the biblical authors, of the fluidity of human groupings and their canons of self-identity, which depend on kinship, language, geography, history, and other factors in varying proportions. There are no neatly divided or permanently stable "nations" in the real world. A sense of this complexity is conveyed by reference not simply to "all the nations" (itself a common biblical phrase), but to "peoples and tribes and languages and nations."

United in Challenging God (Genesis 11:1-9)

The enigmatic story of the building of the Tower of Babel envisages the last moment at which humanity was entirely at one. But they seek to secure this unity by overstepping the limits of the created condition. The tower that reaches for heaven expresses their aspiration for godlike power and status. The "name" they wish to make for themselves challenges the God whose name is uniquely exalted above all creation. Their sin essentially repeats the primal sin of Adam and Eve who sought to be like God. As the last episode of the primeval history of Genesis 1–11, the story warns that the unity of the human race, which has its source in God, can be authentically sought and found only in the worship of God, not in the arrogant pretension to be God. There is also, in God's words "this is only the beginning of what they will do" (Gen 11:6), a hint that more and worse along the same lines can be expected as human history unfolds.

God takes action to "confuse their language" and "to scatter them abroad over the face of all the earth" (11:7, 9). It looks like judgment, but like many divine judgments it is also a blessing in disguise. After all, it fulfills the command of God to humanity to fill the earth (Gen 1:28), and it results in the situation portrayed, to all appearances quite positively, in Genesis 10. The action God takes enforces the created limits of humanity that make for humanity's good. The multiplicity of places in which humans live and the multiplicity of languages they speak, with all the diversity of human culture that these things entail, are the means for humanity to develop the multiform riches of human achievements of all kinds. Rather than the hubristic uniformity of the construction of the tower, the geographical and cultural diversity of human history is how God prefers people to live. This does not mean that humans are supposed to forget or to renounce their original unity. It means that that unity should be expressed not in suppression of diversity but in fulfillment of it. It means that humans must seek the kind of unity that is appropriate to finite creatures, rather than reaching for the status that is appropriate only to God.

That the linguistic diversity resulting from Babel is fundamentally a human good can be confirmed from the story of the coming of the Spirit at Pentecost in Acts 2. This event has often been seen as a reversal of the judgment at Babel, because, miraculously, everyone in the crowd hears the apostles "in the native language of each" (Acts 2:6). What is certainly reversed is the barrier to communication that languages create, but it is noteworthy that the barrier is not transcended by enabling everyone in the crowd to understand the one language in which the apostles speak. In fact, the apostles had only to speak in two languages, Greek and Aramaic, for virtually all these Jews gathered from throughout the Diaspora to understand them. Greek and Aramaic were the linguae francae of the world, very much like English today. The miracle actually subverts that ordinary human means of breaking through the barriers of diversity. Instead, it affirms the native languages of all the people present.

Symbolically, at Pentecost, the nations scattered from Babel are gathered again, this time to the place where God comes down to them unequivocally in blessing, not in judgment. They find a new form of international community, one that is constituted not by its aspiration to divinity but by its worship of the only God of all the world.

After Babel

The primeval history leaves us with humanity, in all its diversity, populating the whole world. Although this situation is a blessing to humanity, it is far from the goal of God's purpose for his human creatures. The deep-rooted, sinful aspiration to divinity, expressed at Babel just as much as in Eden, still exists. The aspiration has been impeded by God's action at Babel, but not removed. It continues to spoil human life and infects all the achievements of the nations.

How God deals with this, how God heals human evil and brings humanity to the kind of fulfillment he always intended, is, of course, the story the rest of the Bible tells. It starts, remarkably, with Abraham and Sarah, just two people. From the global panorama of Genesis 10, the story narrows to become the very particular story of one human couple. But this particular story also begins with God's promise to Abraham, which will be repeated frequently in Genesis:

I will make of you a great nation, and I will bless you, and make your name great, so that you will be a blessing. I will bless those who bless you, and the one who curses you I will curse, and in you all the families of the earth shall be blessed. (Gen. 12:2-3)[9]

In the first place, this promise announces a new reality in the world of the nations: Abraham's descendants, Israel, a people that does not appear in Genesis 10, uniquely the people that God, starting with Abraham, is going to create for himself. But the goal of God's selection of Abraham from all the nations is wider than Israel. It is the blessing of all the families of the earth. (Note that the term "families" is used in Gen. 10:5, 20, 31.) The reason God creates a new nation in the midst of all the nations detailed in Genesis 10 is so that, thereby, he may bless all those nations.

The Bible's story from Abraham onward is therefore a story of globalization. God's blessing on Abraham himself is to be extended to all the nations and to the ends of the earth. God starts with the particular in order to bless all. Later he will once again start with one particular human, Jesus, a descendant of Abraham, a member of God's people Israel, the one who lived, died, and rose to new life on behalf of all others. In the Gospel, taken to the ends of the earth by the church, Jesus is "globalized." The good news that he has achieved God's purpose for the world reaches all the nations and invites them into the living unity that Jesus himself forms with all who believe in him.

9. On the alternative translations, "in you all the families of the earth shall be blessed" and "by you all the families of the earth shall bless themselves" (NRSV and NRSV margin respectively), see Josef Scharbert, "brk," in *Theological Dictionary of the Old Testament*, ed. G. Johannes Botterweck and Helmer Ringgren, trans. John T. Willis (Grand Rapids: Eerdmans, 1975), 2:297; Jo Bailey Wells, *God's Holy People: A Theme in Biblical Theology*, Journal for the Study of the Old Testament Supplement Series 305 (Sheffield: Sheffield Academic, 2000), pp. 203-6; Claus Westermann, *Genesis 12–36*, trans. John J. Scullion (London: SPCK, 1985), pp. 151-52, who comments: "the reflexive translation ['shall be blessed'] is saying no less than the passive or receptive. When 'the families of the earth bless' themselves 'in Abraham,' i.e. call a blessing on themselves under the invocation of his name . . . , then the obvious presupposition is that they receive the blessing. . . . Where the name of Abraham is spoken in a prayer for blessing, the blessing of Abraham streams forth; it knows no bounds and reaches all the families of the earth" (p. 152). Bailey Wells, on the other hand, stresses the difference between the reflexive and the passive interpretations, both of which are possible, and distinguishes the reflexive interpretation as the meaning within the Hebrew Bible, the passive as the meaning when the promise is appropriated in the New Testament, though she notes that the passive meaning is adopted by the Septuagint (*God's Holy People*, pp. 205-6).

But as well as this story of globalization, the Bible's central story, the Bible knows also a counternarrative. If the former is a narrative of global blessing and salvation, the latter is a narrative of global domination and exploitation. Both narratives begin after Babel, but whereas the first seeks the unity of the human race in the worship of God, the latter seeks it, like the builders of the tower, in the arrogant aspiration to be God. The goal of the counternarrative is the same as that of the builders of the tower, but because it begins after Babel, in the world of humanity scattered and divergent, it proceeds not through common consent and conspiracy but through domination. The counternarrative tells how time after time powerful rulers and nations reach for world domination. They aspire to divinity by subjecting the others. They climb the ziggurat of power in order to rule the world, as God does, from the heavens. Although many empires figure in the counternarrative, it is telling that the paradigm of them all is Babylon. (Babel and Babylon are the same word in Hebrew.) In Babylon the Great, world metropolis and mistress of the world, as the book of Revelation depicts her, we finally see the culmination of what the builders of tower merely began (Gen. 11:6).

Nebuchadnezzar the World Ruler (Daniel 4)

In the book of Daniel king Nebuchadnezzar II, the most famous king of ancient Babylon, serves as a paradigm case of rulers who aspire to godlike, global empire. We have already noticed how he speaks of his subjects as "all peoples, nations, and languages that live throughout the earth" (Dan. 4:1), with allusion to the world as Genesis 10 depicts it. Chapter 4 of Daniel tells a tale that in a strangely powerful and haunting way (haunting perhaps especially for those who know William Blake's picture of Nebuchadnezzar in his bovine state) conveys one of the most persistent biblical messages about power. Here, as elsewhere in Scripture, we learn that God alone is sovereign over all; that God humbles the arrogant and exalts the lowly; that human power, with its penchant for hubris, is easily corrupted into tyranny; that only those may rightly rule who, renouncing any aspiration to divine power and recognizing their essential creaturely solidarity with those they rule, neither exalt themselves to rival God nor assume superiority over those they rule; that they alone can be trusted to exercise their power for the good of the powerless.

In Nebuchadnezzar's dream he sees a tree (4:10-15) that stands in the center of the earth, reaches the sky, and overshadows the whole earth. This is the mythical world tree that appears also in Ezekiel 31 (cf. 17:22-23) and the parables of Jesus (Matt. 13:31-32; Mark 4:31-32), always as a symbol of global power. In Nebuchadnezzar's dream it may well at first sight seem an unambiguously positive image of Nebuchadnezzar's beneficent world empire. It corresponds to Nebuchadnezzar's depiction of himself as "prosperous" (4:4: *ra'anan*),[10] a word that almost always elsewhere refers to trees as "verdant" or "flourishing," sometimes metaphorically to people whose prosperity is like the flourishing of a tree. This usage can be very positive (e.g., Ps. 92:12-13). The tree in Nebuchadnezzar's dream, because it is so flourishing, provides food for all living creatures, shade and shelter for animals and birds (4:12). No doubt this is Nebuchadnezzar's rule as he himself imagines it. In that case, the brutally emphatic command to fell the tree (4:14) comes as a rude shock.

However, a second look at the image of the tree suggests that its flourishing has a more ominous aspect. Tall trees, reaching up to heaven, can symbolize the arrogance of the powerful (Isa. 2:12-13; 10:33-34; Ezek. 31:3-14: in the last case the tree is the world tree and represents Assyria, the predecessor to Nebuchadnezzar's Babylonian Empire). That the tree "reached up to heaven" surely recalls the Tower of Babel (Gen 11:4: "a tower with its top in the heavens"). It is as though Nebuchadnezzar's empire, centered on the great city of Babylon that he had built (Dan 4:29-30) and encompassing all nations (4:1), has resurrected the project of the builders of the tower. For a while it looks to be carrying through that project more successfully.

Nebuchadnezzar thinks and behaves as though he were the highest power there is. This is why his own self-image as the beneficent monarch is only one aspect of the ambivalent image of the tree. What he is condemned for is the pride (4:37; cf. vv. 29-30) that goes with forgetting that only God's sovereignty is absolute and eternal (4:3, 17, 25, 32, 34) and only God has the right to deal with his world as he will (4:17, 35). The narrative more or less takes it for granted that, given this attitude, Nebuchadnezzar has abused his power in high-handed and self-serving ways. But one reference makes this clear: Daniel urges him to repent by acting with justice and showing compassion to the poor and oppressed (4:27). Throughout the Bible, justice and protection for the weakest in society

10. In Dan. 4:4 it occurs in Aramaic; elsewhere in the Hebrew Bible it occurs as a Hebrew word.

are the primary purpose of and justification for political power. The Old Testament, which is ambivalent about monarchy, tolerates or commends it only when the unique power of the monarch is used on behalf of the poor, enabling him to intervene to protect the rights of those too weak to resist the abuse of power by others of the king's subjects (e.g., Psalm 72). When kings or other powerful people do abuse their powers to oppress the weak, this is portrayed as the arrogance of people who think they can do what they wish with impunity and do not reckon with God's sovereign authority (e.g., Psalm 10). Every abuse of power has a whiff of self-deification about it.

This is why God characteristically dethrones the arrogant and puts the lowly into positions of power (4:37, 17; cf. Ezek. 17:24; 1 Sam. 2:3-8; Luke 1:51-52). The latter, until they forget their humble origins, know their power is lent to them by God and remember that they are fundamentally the equals of all their people (Deut. 17:20). Nebuchadnezzar can be made fit to rule only by being humiliated. Since, even after the dream and its interpretation, he fails to recognize his true position under God and alongside his subjects, God must humble him to the level of the humblest of his subjects — the wild animals. The one who exalted himself to heaven must be brought down literally to earth. His assimilation to the animals is carefully stated (4:32-33). He does not become like the fierce predatory beasts that in Daniel's visions symbolize the human rule of the world empires (Dan. 7:3-8). He does not resemble the lion that symbolizes his own empire in Daniel 7:4. He is like the oxen and the birds. There is nothing derogatory in this reference to the animals. Presumably, if an ox could be king, he would be a better one than Nebuchadnezzar at the height of his pride. The ox knows its divine master, whom Nebuchadnezzar must learn to know by sharing the humble status of the ox.

Just as God's judgment at Babel proved good for humanity, so, rather remarkably, God's judgment on Nebuchadnezzar for his self-deifying arrogance is not destructive but redemptive. The story holds open the possibility of human power blessed by God when the powerful know their God-given limits and rule accordingly. We might compare the fact that, among the world empires to which Israel was subject, the Persian Empire is portrayed with much less hostility than the others.[11] Among its charac-

---

11. See the books of Ezra, Nehemiah, and Esther. Isaiah 45:1-13 portrays Cyrus as God's anointed, fulfilling God's purpose for his people, though Cyrus himself is ignorant of this.

teristics was its benevolent tolerance of diversity among the peoples who composed it, of which its policy toward Judah (Ezra 1–7) was an instance.

The image of the world tree reappears in Jesus' parable of the mustard seed. In his unique take on the image, it is from the mustard seed, the humblest of seeds, that the world tree grows (Mark 4:31-32). In its own way, this image is as bizarre and unlikely as the restoration of the lycanthrope Nebuchadnezzar to worldwide sovereignty under the King of heaven. But, more broadly than this, the whole complex of ideas about human and divine power and rule that Daniel 4 expresses has deeply informed the New Testament portrayal of Jesus and his exercise of God's sovereignty over the world. Jesus is the ruler whose kingdom does not reach up to heaven but comes down from heaven. Whereas Nebuchadnezzar had to be forced to share the condition of his lowliest subjects, Jesus voluntarily humbles himself as far as the slave's or the criminal's abandoned death. He is both the divine king who has the uniquely divine right to rule his human subjects and the human king who qualifies for his rule by self-denying solidarity with his human brothers and sisters (Phil 2:5-11). In strictest fulfillment of Daniel 4:17, it is to the lowliest of all that God gives the kingdom. This is a form of globalization as far from domination as one could get.

At the Hub of the Global Market (Ezekiel 26–28)

The great superpowers of the ancient Middle East — Egypt, Assyria, Babylon, Persia, the Hellenistic empires, and Rome — are the Bible's paradigms of the global power that rests on military might and takes political form. But there is another sort of global power for which a different empire, a purely economic one, paradigmatically stands. This is Tyre, the city whose economic dominance is denounced in three remarkable chapters of Ezekiel's prophecy (26–28).[12]

The list of some forty peoples and places with whom Tyre traded (27:1-25)[13] reminds us again of the Table of the Nations in Genesis 10. Some names are common, others are different, but the global reach is comparable: from Spain (Tarshish) in the west to Persia in the east, from Armenia

---

12. See also Isaiah 23.

13. 27:3-11 is a poetic description of Tyre imagined as a great and resplendent ship, while 27:12-25 is a more prosaic account of Tyre's international trade.

(Beth-togarmah) in the north to southern Arabia (Sheba) in the south. For all these places Tyre was the middleman,[14] facilitating world trade, creating, we might say, a global market. In this way Tyre enriched "many peoples," but especially, we should notice, the powerful elites: "the kings of the earth" (27:33). But, of course, Tyre's role at the hub of world trade especially enriched Tyre herself (28:4-5), and with wealth grew arrogance (28:5), that self-deifying hubris that drives conquerors, emperors, and multinational executives alike. It is not clear in what exactly "the unrighteousness of your trade" consisted (28:18), but "violence" (28:16) suggests more than corrupt dealings, perhaps piracy, perhaps brutal enforcement of excise duties. In any case, there is certainly the implication that Tyre's extraordinary economic success goes to her head: she thinks she can get away with anything. Her downfall is all the more unexpected and shocking (27:32-36). She sinks like one of her own ships, grossly overloaded with stuff (27:25-28).

The Destroyers of the Earth[15] (Revelation)

The Bible's narrative of globalization by domination and exploitation culminates in the book of Revelation's vividly imaginative portrayal of the Roman Empire. As well as the dragon, representing the diabolical power inspiring the system, there are three main symbols of earthly and globalizing power: the beast with seven heads, the second beast or false prophet, and Babylon the great city, the harlot. The seven-headed beast is the political power of the empire acquired and maintained by military domination. The false prophet is the political religion of the empire, the imperial cult, which maintains the power of the empire by ideology and propaganda. Babylon is the city of Rome, growing rich on the spoils of empire and worldwide trade.

One remarkable fact about Revelation's portrayal of this global system of domination is the pervasive allusion to Old Testament prophecy, which conveys the sense that Rome and her empire are the culmination of all the evil empires of history. The beast takes its place in the sequence of terrifying monsters that represent the world empires (from Nebuchadnezzar's Babylon onward) in Daniel's vision (Dan. 7:2-8), summing up in

---

14. Note the alternation of references to imports and to exports in 27:12-24.
15. The phrase is from Rev. 11:18.

itself the destructive qualities of them all (Rev. 13:1-8). In the vision of Babylon the great harlot and the oracle of destruction against her (Revelation 17–18), there are allusions to every one of the Old Testament's prophetic oracles against Babylon, as well as the two great oracles against Tyre (Isaiah 23; Ezekiel 26–28).[16] In fact, Revelation's Babylon is just as much a reincarnation of Old Testament Tyre as she is of Old Testament Babylon, and so represents Rome's economic dominance and exploitation, just as much as her military and political domination. Moreover, it is not difficult to see that her genealogy goes right back to Babel, and while there is no clear echo of that story, there may well be an ironic allusion in the statement that Babylon's "sins are heaped high as heaven" (Rev. 18:5).[17] In Babylon's attempt to acquire divine status, only her sins reach heaven, whereas her opposite number, the new Jerusalem, comes down from heaven (Rev. 21:2, 10).

Thus, in chapter 13, Rome's power is portrayed as a marauding monster. The empire had survived a crisis in which it came close to collapse, and its survival (the healing of the beast's mortal wound) made it seem indestructible. Its deification was not only a matter of propaganda from the center but also the spontaneous response of all who observed its sheer, unchallengeable might: "they worshiped the beast, saying, 'Who is like the beast and who can fight against it?' " (Rev. 13:4). This is worship of power. But the beast also has a highly effective propaganda machine, the false prophet, which promotes the ideology of Roman power. According to the propaganda, Rome's conquests have bestowed great benefits on the world, the famous *pax Romana*. Her subjects are thereby duped into welcoming rather than resisting the empire. But the empire appears in its true colors as the rampaging monster of John's vision.

The harlot Babylon, in chapter 17, is the city of Rome, unmistakably because she is seated on seven hills (Rev. 17:9). It is important to realize that the metaphor of prostitution does not here refer to false religion, as it does when, in the Old Testament prophets, it characterizes Israel as God's faithless, promiscuous wife. Babylon is not God's wife. Rather prostitution here stands for trade, as it does in Isaiah's oracle about Tyre (Isa. 23:15-18) and Nahum's about Nineveh (Nah. 3:4). But whereas Tyre's profits came from being the middleman of world trade, Rome was where all the goods of the empire (and beyond) ended up. It

16. There are echoes also of Old Testament oracles against Edom.
17. The primary allusion here is to Jer. 51:9.

was for the city's own massive consumption of staples and extravagant luxuries alike that Rome exploited her empire economically (see the very accurately representative list of Rome's imports in Rev. 18:12-13). This is what Revelation calls the harlot Babylon's "fornication" with "the kings of the earth" (Rev. 17:2; cf. 18:3, 9). The phrase occurred also with reference to Tyre in Ezekiel (27:33); in Revelation it recognizes that those outside Rome who did well for themselves out of her trade were the local elites in the provinces of the empire, as well as the shipowners and merchants (Rev. 18:15-19), not the common people. Finally, the inhuman exploitation that this economic system entailed is highlighted by the emphatic way that the list of imports to Babylon ends: "bodies, that is, human lives" (Rev. 18:13: a literal translation). "Bodies" is what slaves were commonly called, mere carcasses bought and sold in the slave markets as property like other consumer goods. Here it is pointed out that actually they are human beings.

At the height of her prosperity Babylon boasted: "I rule as a queen; I am no widow, and I will never see grief" (Rev. 18:7). This is the illusion of prosperity from which Ezekiel's Tyre also suffered. In literal fact it reproduces Rome's boast of being the eternal city. It is another form of self-deification: the system that feeds and fulfills the consumerist dream is the culmination of history and can be trusted to go on for ever.

Rome claimed to rule the whole inhabited world, a claim so patently untrue (the Parthian Empire was a massive presence to Rome's east) that only those duped by propaganda or by their own infatuation with power could have believed it. The emphatically universal language of Revelation — all the inhabitants of the earth worship the beast (13:3), Babylon is the great city that rules over the kings of the earth (17:18), and all nations have drunk of her wine (18:3) — corresponds to Rome's claims and reflects the globalizing thrust of all such superpowers. But it can also be seen as pointing beyond Rome to later beasts and later Babylons, for whom there would be wider vistas of global opportunity. I do not mean that Revelation predicts one specific superpower, the mother of all superpowers, in the last period of history. That is not the kind of prophecy Revelation is. But the way that Revelation's images of evil gather up so many of the Old Testament precedents into something like a culminating case of global domination and exploitation suggests to me that they refer to Rome, not just in the very concrete character of the empire in which Revelation's first readers lived, but also as a model of where all such globalizing enterprises lead.

Jesus and the Kingdom of God

In many Old Testament passages, like the Psalms we quoted earlier, there is no doubt that the dominion of God over his whole creation is a present reality, but the prophets also look forward to the day when "the LORD shall become king over all the earth" (Zech. 14:9). The latter relates to the acceptance of God's rule by all people. The God known to Israel as her God will become the God of all the nations. A kind of globalization of God's rule is envisaged, one that characteristically has a particular starting point in Israel and in Jesus, whose role as Messiah is to enable Israel's vocation to be a light to all the nations.

When Jesus spoke of the kingdom of God he undoubtedly had this global future in mind. We have already mentioned the parable of the mustard seed, in which Jesus makes use of the image of the world tree:

> With what can we compare the kingdom of God, or what parable will we use for it? It is like a mustard seed, which, when sown upon the ground, is the smallest of all the seeds on earth; yet when it is sown it grows up and becomes the greatest of all shrubs, and puts forth large branches, so that the birds of the air can make nests in its shade. (Mark 4:30-32)

Jesus contrasts the smallest of all seeds (as the mustard seed was proverbially thought to be) with the greatest of all shrubs into which it grows. But the sizeable shrub that the mustard plant actually is is so described as to suggest the mythical world tree that overshadows the whole world. In Ezekiel the birds that nest in its branches represent the nations that enjoy the blessings of God's global kingdom (Ezek. 17:23; cf. 31:6). Characteristically Jesus expands a matter of common observation by his hearers into a way of talking about what God is doing in Jesus' ministry and in the global future.

The point of the parable is not to focus on the process of growth but to contrast the apparently insignificant beginnings with the astonishingly great end result. The modern ideology of progress tricks us into thinking all too easily of a steadily cumulative process by which either the church's missionary outreach or the values of the kingdom of God spread around the globe. But while there is, in God's purpose, a movement from the particular to the universal, a globalizing dynamic to his rule, there is no reason to see this as a single process that, even if there are also setbacks, generally progresses in a cumulative way. The hand of God in history cannot be plotted and calculated in such a way. Jesus' concern in the parable is rather to suggest that, insignificant as the signs of the kingdom occurring in Jesus' ministry might seem, especially from a global perspective, in fact they really are the start of what will finally prove to be God's global rule.

If reference to the kingdom of God invokes the Bible's narrative of globalization, it is the globalization of blessing and salvation that is in view, not the globalization of domination and exploitation. Use of the image of "kingdom" or "rule" may rather easily obscure this difference, but there is much in the Gospels to suggest that Jesus was at pains to avoid the impression that God rules in the way earthly rulers do. It is a striking fact that, while Jesus speaks frequently of "the kingdom of God," he never calls God "king,"[18] and that in his parables (which often begin, "The kingdom of God is like this") it is only rarely that a king appears as the figure who represents God.[19] Thus Jesus' use of the term "kingdom of God" connects his teaching with the prophets and with later Jewish expectation of the coming of God's universal rule, but by avoiding the concrete image of God as king and preferring other images, notably Father, he shifts the focus much more to characterizing God's rule as radically different from that of earthly rulers. The issue is not just that God's rule should replace the rule of the pagan empires, nor even just that God's righteous rule should replace the oppressive rule of the pagan empires, as many of Jesus' Jewish contemporaries hoped. More radically, Jesus wishes to portray God's rule as an alternative to earthly rule that is quite unlike all earthly rule.

The image of kingship — despite the Old Testament ideal of the king who secures justice for the oppressed — was hard to rescue from the sense of exploitative domination (see Mark 10:42). In the parables Jesus subverts expectations of kings and masters and employers by making the story turn on their surprising actions (e.g., Matt. 18:23-27; 20:1-15; Luke 12:37). Outside the parables, Jesus avoids calling God "king" and privileges instead the other common Jewish description of God: "Father." The parabolic saying with which Jesus comments on the temple tax (the tax levied by the Jewish theocracy in God's name) is instructive: "From whom do the kings of the earth take toll and tribute? from their own children or from others?" (Matt. 17:25). The parallel, which for Jesus illustrates God's relationship with his people, is not with the way earthly kings treat their subjects (they tax them) but with the way earthly kings treat their own children (they do

---

18. The only exception is Matt. 5:35, a quotation from Ps. 48:2.
19. Only Matt. 18:23-34; 22:1-13; cf. Luke 19:12.

not tax them). The point is not that earthly fathers may not be oppressive, but that fathers function differently in relation to their family from the way kings function in relation to their subjects. Whereas the ancient political rhetoric of the king as father to his people would have meant little to Jesus' hearers, struggling to make a living and aware of government primarily as aggravating that struggle through taxation, the image of the father as generously providing for his children had reality (Luke 11:11-13). Whereas the king in the parable of the unforgiving servant acts as no one would expect a king to behave, the father in the parable of the prodigal son acts in a way that is just about understandable (though not expected) in a father, but would be incomprehensible in a king.

Related to this is the kind of social group Jesus expects his disciples to be, since they are the group who already live under the rule of God and instantiate its presence in the world. That they are to form a "contrast society" (contrasting with many accepted ways and values) is evident in various ways, but for our purpose the extent to which Jesus fashions a radical alternative to domination is especially noteworthy:

> You know that among the Gentiles those whom they recognize as their rulers lord it over them, and their great ones are tyrants over them. But it is not so among you; but whoever wishes to be great among you must be your servant, and whoever wishes to be first among you must be slave of all. (Mark 10:42-44; cf. Luke 22:25-26; Matt. 23:11)

Echoes of this theme are found in several places in the Gospels, but most important is the scene in John 13, where Jesus himself adopts the role of the slave by washing his disciples' feet. Washing feet, a frequent, everyday menial task, was, more definitely and exclusively than any other task, the role of the slave. It was what every free person axiomatically regarded as unthinkably beneath their dignity. Jesus enjoins the disciples to wash one another's feet (13:14) not as a mere symbol of humility and not, as sometimes suggested, as a religious rite, but as a concrete instance, the most telling possible, of how the disciples should relate to each other. The ordinary everyday requirement of washing feet they are to do for each other. If this is not beneath their dignity, nothing is.

Also relevant are the ways in which Jesus in the Gospels envisages the role of his disciples in the future. Their mission is certainly to be universal: "the good news must first be proclaimed to all nations" (Mark 13:10); "make disciples of all nations" (Matt. 28:19). But their role is not so much to achieve the universal coming of the kingdom as to proclaim it. They are to announce the coming of God's rule, to witness to it in signs, as Jesus did, to recruit disciples to the communities that God's rule itself creates as it comes.

Finally, there is a general feature of Jesus' ministry as portrayed in the Gospels that is usually taken for granted, but merits attention in the context of this essay. It is the small-scale particularity of so much of what happens. The kingdom of God is a concept that projects a universal horizon, but in Jesus' understanding it never overrides or obscures the particular. God's rule takes effect in Jesus' healings and exorcisms, in which specific individuals are restored to well-being, and in Jesus' very concrete personal association with all kinds of particular people. The story of Jesus is a collection of little stories, mostly about the sort of people who scarcely ever appear in historical accounts from the ancient world, because, compared with the movers and shakers of history, they were insignificant. The notion of globalization requires us to think in terms of the big picture, but God's movement from the particular to the universal, the story of the globalization of blessing and salvation, never leaves the particular behind. Real individual people, living communities of people, the concrete reality of their daily lives, are not dispensable for the sake of the grand scheme. If there is a grand scheme, it is precisely for their sake.

The Witnesses of Jesus (Revelation)

We could explore the theme of the church's worldwide mission in other New Testament literature, but within the limits of this essay it is important to return to Revelation, because there we see — it is a central theme of the book — how the two narratives of globalization contrast and clash.

The key words are "witness" and "conquer" — images drawn from the law court and the battlefield respectively. Both have Jesus and his followers as their subject, while only the second has the beast also as its subject. There is, however, a bestial counterpart to witness — "deceive." Revelation makes much use of the themes of truth and deceit. Jesus himself is "the faithful and true witness" (3:14; cf. 1:5) because of the witness he bore to God during his earthly life and his faithfulness in maintaining that witness even at the cost of his life. Jesus' followers are also "witnesses" (17:6; cf. 2:13); more specifically they are those who bear "the witness of Jesus" (12:17; 19:10). This phrase does not mean "witness to Jesus," but the witness that Jesus bore to God and that Christians continue to bear. This witness by Jesus and his followers to the true God and his righteousness serves to expose the falsehood of the beast's idolatry, his assertion of his own power as ultimate and divine. The "witness of Jesus" exposes this idolatry because the beast's power cannot overcome it, not even when it puts the witnesses to death. Quite the opposite, in their deaths Jesus and the martyrs witness to God's truth by not denying it even in the face of death.

When Revelation uses the image of messianic war, it certainly intends nothing in the least militaristic on the part of Jesus and his followers. Rather, it is by their faithful witness even, should it be necessary, at the cost of their lives that the followers of Jesus share in his own victory over evil and play their part in the coming of God's kingdom (12:11). Inevitably, they are involved in a "war" with the beast, which on his side involves brute force as well as propaganda, but on their side is fought purely by nonviolent witness. When their witness proves convincing, the beast's deceits are exposed and people are won from serving the beast to worshiping the true God. Very revealing is the fact that the deaths of the martyrs, understood as witness, can be described both as the beast's victory over them (11:7; 13:7) and as their victory over the beast (15:2). From the beast's earthbound perspective he seems to have defeated them, but from the heavenly perspective that the book of Revelation allows its readers to share it is they who have won the real victory.

For our purposes in this essay what is most important is that the way in which followers of Jesus serve God's globalizing purpose of blessing and salvation for the world is by noncoercive witness to the truth. (Revelation stresses verbal witness, along with the suffering that results, but it also describes Christians as "those who keep the commandments of God and hold the testimony of Jesus" [12:17]. Their lives of obedience to God certainly assist their witness.) Because of the witness of Jesus' followers, a people he has redeemed "from every tribe and language and people and nation" (5:9) so that they may bear witness to "the people and tribes and languages and nations" (11:9), the book of Revelation holds out a real hope for the conversion of the nations to God. Triumphant over the beast in heaven, the martyrs sing: "All nations will come and worship before you" (15:4).

Consequent Reflections on Contemporary Globalization

Globalization is a multivalent notion. Many aspects of contemporary globalization, such as the speed of communication and travel, are historically unprecedented and not to be found in the biblical material we have discussed. Nevertheless there are important continuities, and doubtless, in some sort of hermeneutical circle, my awareness of contemporary globalization has already influenced the way I have read and presented the biblical material in this essay.

The biblical material suggests that human society and history have an inherent orientation toward the global that stems from the fundamental unity of the human race and its limitation to a common home on the earth. Ancient Israel's world may seem rather small to us, but it is notable how frequently the Scriptures that took shape within it open that world to its farthest known limits. Those Scriptures are alert to the complex economic, cultural, and political interconnections of that world, and they cannot, it seems, envisage a future destiny for Israel that does not also involve the nations. Even more importantly (and however Israel's faith in one God may have developed, historically, behind the texts), the God of the Hebrew Scriptures is not the God of Israel alone, but the Creator and Lord of the whole creation and all the nations. To think of this God is to think globally. But the Hebrew Scriptures go much further than this in envisaging a globalizing process: a divine purpose to bring blessing and salvation to all the nations in a way that started with Israel but is by no means intended to stop at Israel.

With such a background in the Scriptures of Israel, it should not be surprising that the New Testament, beginning with God's most particular presence in the world in the person of Jesus the Jew, projects a universal horizon for the salvation Jesus brings. The good news of Jesus, Savior of the world, and of the coming of God's rule in all the world, is of universal relevance and significance. His international people, the church, drawn from all the nations, has the commission to enlighten all the nations with this message.

The inescapably global dimension of human existence means that there is also another kind of globalizing impulse, one that is tainted by human sin. Indeed, as the Bible portrays it, it is driven by the primal and fundamental sin: the human desire to usurp divinity and achieve some sort of ultimate power and status for humans, an escape from finitude. This is idolatry. Inevitably its result is not the common good, but the domination of some, the powerful, over others.

That globalization risks idolatry can be seen very clearly in the contemporary world. The recent process of globalization has been driven by a very definite goal: the economic goal of a completely unfettered free market for the exchange of goods and commodities across all national borders. For the sake of this goal all other considerations can and should be overridden, because the free market is seen as the way of meeting all human needs. This is the latest version of the modern idea of progress, a metanarrative of salvation by the unrestricted pursuit of material wealth.

Like all idolatries, this one has turned out to be an ideology of domination: "Globalization has so far functioned predominantly as an enhanced opportunity for the economic, political and cultural outreach of the powerful."[20] It may have produced more wealth in aggregate worldwide, but in such a way that the rich have grown richer and the poorest poorer: "growing inequality is the most striking feature of the global economy."[21] This is economic growth at the expense of the poor. It is also at the expense of all other values in human life: face-to-face community, social solidarity, uncommercialized cultural diversity, and the preservation of the environment.

One way biblical faith comes into its own, even in the godless world of global economics and international politics, is in its critique of idolatry. A corollary of faith in the biblical God is alertness to every tendency to exalt something of the created world to the status that belongs only to God. Such tendencies are endemic in human life and need to be constantly exposed. When the failures of economic globalization — such as the failure to improve the lot of the very poor — are met with the explanation that the de-restriction of markets has not yet gone far enough and that poor countries are to blame for impeding the free play of market economics, we must surely suspect that the theory has become an idol.

Much of contemporary Western society has been deeply infected with the belief that economic growth is the supreme good. There are other widely acknowledged values, to be sure, such as tolerance and respect for all, and the right of each to pursue happiness in their own chosen way, but economic growth seems to be necessary for the others to have any real substance. It is doubtful whether there is much precedent in history for such a scale of values in society at large (as distinct from the few who have always made their own economic aggrandizement their priority in life), but perhaps it would be most at home at the court and in the merchants' quarters of ancient Tyre.

20. Frank Turner, "Globalisation from a Pastoral-Theological Viewpoint," *New Blackfriars* 86 (2005): 172-84, here 184.
21. Ian Linden, "A New Map of the World," *New Blackfriars* 86 (2005): 144-55, here 146.

The Bible certainly has one economic preoccupation, but it is with the plight of the poorest, the truly destitute. A core Christian criterion to assess any global development must be: does it benefit or further disadvantage the world's poorest people? This is a priority for the church because it is the biblical God's priority and an essential implication of God's love for all people. Love for all people requires special attention to the most needy.

So what of the contemporary church in a globalized world? It has to be said, first, that one of the great tragedies of church history has been a recurrent confusion of the church's mission with movements of global domination. Too often the church has appeared to ride on the back of the seven-headed beast, and in the modern era of imperialism and colonialism Christianity has not surprisingly been seen, all too often, as an aspect of Western aggrandizement and exploitation. In most recent history, radical Islamism has all too readily been able to portray Western dominance over the Islamic world as that of Christian over Muslim, and the indigenous Christians in Muslim countries have borne the brunt of this perception. (Their sacrificial loyalty to Christ has been a witness of incalculable value.)

Western missionaries have too often exported the peculiarly Western trappings of British, European, or American Christianity, but it can also be said that over the long course of Christian history the gospel has taken root in a remarkably varied range of cultural contexts and borne fruit of similarly rich cultural diversity. The Bible, as we have seen, does value the diversity of human languages, histories, and cultures. The way such diversity is affected by globalization is complex. Some see "glocalization" occurring as a reaction to globalization, and it is apparent that globalization produces richly multicultural societies as well as the homogenization that derives especially from the dominance of American popular culture throughout the world. In these circumstances the church must be true to its character as a rainbow people, called by God from "every tribe and language and people and nation" in order to witness to "every tribe and language and people and nation."

The universal church, supposing it can truly recognize its essential unity in diversity, is the most international of all human communal identities. (Its international spread is greater than that of Islam or Buddhism.) Its potential as a movement for resisting the evils of global domination and promoting instead a global solidarity of the prosperous with the needy and of the more fortunate with the more threatened (by climate change, for example) must be unparalleled. Its profile as such a movement by no means prejudices its mission to announce the good news of Jesus and the coming of God's kingdom, because such forms of global solidarity reflect what human life under the rule of God should be. The Bible's polarity between the globalization of domination and the globalization of blessing confronts believers with many concrete choices that must be made in our contemporary context.

CHAPTER 5

Freedom and Belonging

Freedom is a hugely potent word, especially in our contemporary world. It could plausibly be claimed that freedom is *the* primary value of modernity, and that postmodernity, while changing many things, has certainly not changed that. Of the three components of the slogan of the French Revolution — liberty, equality, and fraternity — it is liberty that has worn best and come to be most widely valued. But this is not to say that freedom always means the same thing. Big words like that rarely do. Isaiah Berlin said that the meaning of freedom "is so porous that there is little interpretation that it seems able to resist."[1] It is a potent, even a magic word, but one that for that very reason can also be dangerous.

There is a quite widely perceived contemporary problem about the compatibility of freedom and community — between the human need to be independent and the human need to belong. The increase in both the desire and the concrete opportunities for individual freedom — along with doubtless other connected factors, such as increased mobility — has led to an atomized society, in which community is no longer a given context of relationships in which individuals find themselves embedded, but results only from the free choice of individuals to associate. Most people want to belong, but many experience this as in tension with the desire for freedom, and contemporary cultural and economic factors give a strong advantage, in this tension, to individual freedom. Community loses out.

Is freedom necessarily destructive of community? Does community necessarily inhibit freedom? Must we be content with some kind of un-

---

1. Quoted in John Webster, *Barth's Moral Theology* (Edinburgh: T&T Clark, 1998), p. 100.

easy balance between the two? Or does the dilemma result from particular construals of freedom and community in modern Western culture? Are there ways of understanding and practicing freedom that actually enable community rather than destroying community? I would argue that there are resources in the Bible and the Christian tradition for constructing a positive interrelationship between freedom and belonging.

It seems that freedom conceived as opposed to belonging, exalted as a value purely in itself, leads not only to the destruction of community but also to the distortion of freedom itself. But this is an aspect of a wider point: that, in a pluralistic society like the modern West, there is a real danger of freedom becoming the only common value, and that, if this happens, freedom will be seriously distorted, even destroyed, because freedom only really flourishes for human good when it is valued in a context of other prime values and virtues. A so-called freedom-loving society will be no more than a jungle of competing interests unless it values other goods as well as freedom. The pioneers of modern democracy, in the United States and elsewhere, took this for granted, but we can no longer afford just to assume it.

Since freedom is such a big word — susceptible to so many interpretations and uses — we need to consider a variety of kinds of freedom that have become culturally dominant in the modern and contemporary periods in the West (and exported to other parts of the world).

Democratic Freedoms

Since the rest of what I say about the legacy of the European Enlightenment, the culture of modernity, will be mostly critical, I want to stress at the outset the positive aspects of freedom that the Enlightenment has bequeathed to us. The Enlightenment insisted, with some degree of novelty, on the rights of the individual over against the power of society or the state. Ideas of the dignity of the individual and the fundamental human rights of the individual that must be universally respected took their modern form through the Enlightenment, though arguably they have roots in the Christian tradition. The notion of human rights, though it is probably not a matter of self-evident universal values, as the Enlightenment believed, has proved very useful legally and internationally. Some people now associate talk of rights with contemporary hyperindividualism and the decline of social obligation — rights without responsibilities — but this is the fault not of the idea of human rights itself, but of the decay of a wider context of values.

Freedom from All Limits

However, modern concepts of freedom range much more widely than those that are enshrined in democratic political systems. In the spirit of modernity there is an aspiration to absolute freedom or freedom from all limits whatever. A famous and remarkable passage from the fifteenth-century philosopher Pico della Mirandola will illustrate this well. Pico imagines God addressing Adam, just after he has created him:

> "The nature of other creatures, which has been determined, is confined within the bounds prescribed by us. You, who are confined by no limits, shall determine for yourself your own nature, in accordance with your own free will, in whose hand I have placed you. . . . We have made you neither heavenly nor earthly, neither mortal nor immortal, so that, more freely and more honourably the moulder and maker of yourself, you may fashion yourself in whatever form you shall prefer."
>
> [Pico continues] O sublime generosity of God the Father! O Highest and most wonderful felicity of man! To him it was granted to have what he chooses, to be what he wills.[2]

This is a portrait of humanity as the creature with no given limits, absolutely self-determining, able to choose what it will be — in effect, self-creating. What Pico has really done in this passage, following the tendency of the Italian Renaissance to treat humanity as a god, is this: he has transferred to human beings a theological understanding of God as the absolutely self-determining reality. It says something about the continuity of this notion of human freedom from the Renaissance through the Enlightenment that Pico does more or less what in the early nineteenth century Ludwig Feuerbach advocated. For Feuerbach our ideas of God are just projections of human qualities and potentialities. We need to reclaim our humanity by rejecting the transcendent God and reappropriating for humanity our own true divinity. This is what Pico was doing, except that he did not give up

---

2. Quoted in Delwin Brown, *To Set at Liberty: Christian Faith and Human Freedom* (Maryknoll, N.Y.: Orbis, 1981), p. 6.

belief in God. What he effectively gave up was the finiteness of humans as finite creatures, investing humanity with the infinite freedom to transcend all limits that theology had attributed to God.

One cannot deny that the rejection of given limits in the project of modernity was genuinely liberating in important ways. It rescued people from fatalism — from simply acquiescing in whatever is the case out of a general conviction that nothing can really be changed. It gave huge energy to the project of improving human life and its conditions. But it had a Promethean tendency — a tendency to suppose that all given limits can be transcended and abolished. We have seen the downside of this understanding of freedom in the ecological crisis, which in many ways has been a very hard lesson in learning that there simply are given limits in the nature of things, and that humanity's too-Promethean attempts to disregard these have been reckless and ignorant, bringing on disasters that no one foresaw. But the rejection of human finiteness, the understanding of freedom as an ability, even a right to break out of all restrictions, to recognize no limits, has been very damaging also when adopted as an idea of individual freedom.

Modern individuals came to think that the more freedom they have the better and that the freedom they wanted was self-determination. For this understanding of freedom other people can only be restrictions on my freedom. Society becomes a sort of contract in which we promise not to exercise our own freedom to the extent of impinging on other people's freedom. John Stuart Mill's famous definition encapsulates this notion:

> The only freedom which deserves the name is that of pursuing our own good in our own way, so long as we do not attempt to deprive others of theirs, or impede their efforts to attain it.[3]

Freedom here is something the individual exercises as an independent individual. It has no positive relationship to anyone else's freedom. Essentially it sees freedom as competitive. On this definition of freedom my freedom really would be increased if I denied other people their freedom, overruled their freedom, subjected them to my will. For someone really driven by this kind of freedom other people simply get in the way. For society to be possible at all, according to Mill's argument, we have in fact

---

3. Quoted in Alessandro Passerin d'Entrèves, *The Notion of the State* (Oxford: Clarendon, 1967), pp. 204-5.

to restrict our freedom, to compromise our own freedom in order to allow others theirs. But this restriction of the individual's freedom is precisely a *restriction*. We would be able to be more free if it weren't for other people. So freedom and society pull in different directions.

This is where we first see the incompatibility of freedom and community. On this view of freedom obligations to other people restrict it. Accordingly, the lowest-common-denominator morality of contemporary Western culture puts obligation to others in an entirely negative form: Do what you like so long as you don't harm anyone else. This is what we are left with if freedom for the individual is understood as transcending all limits and if freedom is the only common value left in a pluralistic society.

Freedom as Maximal Independence

Modern individualistic freedom is in full-scale revolt against the given. This means not only that it accepts no given limits, or does so only grudgingly, as a concession. It also means that freedom is conceived as complete independence. That is, it rejects dependence. Freedom is not received from others or enhanced by others. Freedom is an inherent capacity that the individual deploys in an exercise of self-creation. Each has, in Pico della Mirandola's words, the freedom to choose who they will be.

This kind of freedom as maximal independence makes people unwilling to make long-term commitments or to stick with relationships or situations that are not going well. People want the right to move on. They want to keep their options open. They hate being dependent on others because it is restrictive. All these facets of freedom are antithetical to community, which requires such old-fashioned virtues as faithfulness and commitment. Or, to put it another way: maximal independence is incompatible with belonging. Of course, people still want to belong, but contemporary people experience the desire to belong as in considerable tension with freedom. They get divorced and then they regret it. Or they want lifelong loving commitment to a partner, but feel it would be unbearably restrictive actually to marry. Family relationships are obvious victims of freedom as maximal independence, but neighborliness is another. Even spirituality is affected: private versions of new age spirituality leave one freer than so-called institutional religion that requires commitment and obligation.

Lest we think of this solely in terms of attitudes in people's minds, we should note that economic factors play a role: it is hard to belong when you have to keep moving from one job to another or from one place to another. How many people now have neighbors they have known all their lives or colleagues they have worked with all their career, as most people did not so long ago?

Freedom as Consumer Choice

Alongside freedom as maximal independence, the other dominant aspect of freedom in contemporary Western culture is freedom of consumer choice. Having choice can certainly be a good thing. Even rather trivial forms of choice make life more enjoyable. But we may well wonder whether our society has not gone about as far as it can in simply multiplying choice in every aspect of life that can be bought. Consumer choice certainly can be a means of commercial manipulation cloaking itself in the illusion of freedom. But probably the worst manifestation of a consumer culture occurs when the model of consumer choice is applied to things other than those we purchase, such as choosing our moral values.

The effect of a culture that overvalues consumer choice is to give the impression that freedom is really enhanced by the mere multiplication of choices, regardless of how we exercise choice. What matters is having the choice, not making the right choice, not choosing well or rightly. This is one of the points where one may fear that freedom is becoming the only value. Distinguishing good choices and bad choices is serious when there are accepted notions of good and bad. In a culture that socializes people into a range of values and virtues that constitute good life, the main value of choice will be that it enables the making of good choices. Freedom is a faculty for, choice is an opportunity for *the good*. But without a widely accepted range of values and virtues, choice becomes the good that is valued in and of itself.

Freedom as Domination?

A question that must always be raised about freedom is whether it has domination as its corollary. In other words, is it freedom for some at the expense of others? Is it the freedom the master enjoys only because he has slaves? It is easy for us to see that ancient Athenian democracy was possible for the free citizens of Athens only because their slaves and their wives did all the work and left them the free time to engage in the debates and decisions of direct democracy. Modern democracy was for a long time really a kind of plutocracy, in the sense that there was a property qualification for voting. Universal franchise came late in the day. The economic relationships that free some while enslaving others are not always so obvious, but there are always economic aspects to freedom. What is happening in a democracy where the poor have the vote but few of them actually turn out to vote? How far does consumer choice in the West depend on cheap labor, not to mention child labor, in parts of the developing world?

We have already observed that for freedom conceived as maximal independence for the individual, other people appear only as restrictions on the freedom of the individual. But we also have to press, in some cases, a harder critique: are freedoms we value ourselves only possible because others are denied freedoms?

Freedom, we have to conclude, is such a *magic* word, such an alluring notion, that it is also a powerfully ideological word — in the bad sense of "ideology," meaning that it mystifies a situation we would dislike or be ashamed of if we saw it more clearly. Freedom can cloak oppression and justify selfishness. It covers a multitude of goods and a multitude of evils and a lot of rather ambiguous things. It deserves a lot more critical *attention* than our society usually affords it, while priding itself precisely on its freedom.

Beyond Hyperindividualism — Reciprocity

As resources for constructing a notion of freedom that can serve as an adequate alternative to the kinds of freedom that in the contemporary world are proving inimical to human flourishing, there are two motifs that I draw from my understanding of the Bible and the Christian tradition: that freedom is finite and that freedom is relational.

Freedom is finite. This means, partly, that it is given, just as for finite creatures all goods are received. Freedom is given ultimately by God, but also in the concrete circumstances of life it is given by social structures and traditions and by other people. We do not simply win freedom for our individual selves; we receive it. We grant freedom to each other (or fail to do so); we enhance each other's freedom (or suppress it). In a well-functioning community we are not restrictions on each other's freedom, but enable each other's freedom. Freedom is not a zero-sum game, such that the more freedom I have the less you have. The more freedom we give each other the more we all have.

If we are given freedom by others, then it is a mistake to want a kind of independence that excludes any sort of dependence. The independence of finite creatures is always rooted in their more fundamental dependence on God. But the same is, less absolutely, true of our dependence on other people. Children grow to independence from the dependence they have on adults, and are forever indebted to those adults for the independence they acquire. But adult independence is also really always only an aspect of the complex web of interdependence that human society is. Moreover, in the context of current ecological threats, it is vital to recover a lively sense of human dependence on the rest of the natural world. Human independence is rooted in dependence on nature, just as all creaturely existence is rooted in dependence on God the Creator.

That freedom is finite also means that it has limits. It is the condition of a finite creature to live within limits. But of course finite creatures are created such as to find fulfillment within limits. Limits belong to the good of finite creatures. I would not be happier if I could be in two hundred places at the same time, because I have not been made to find happiness in such a capacity. This does not mean that we can always know in advance where we shall find the limits to be (could humans, for example, colonize Mars?), but we should not find the very idea of limits alien and restrictive, and so we should be open to discovering limits at the same time as we may discover new possibilities. In other words, we must abandon that element in the modern spirit that aspired to the limitless freedom appropriate only to God. Feuerbach was wrong: in the concept of God we recognize necessary distinctions between God and ourselves; we recognize ourselves to be finite, not infinite.

Freedom is finite, and it is also relational. That means: not only do we give and receive freedom, but furthermore freedom is fulfilled in being freedom *for*. The contemporary concept of freedom is deficient in having no real idea of what freedom is for. When freedom is the only value, it becomes no more than having the choice to do whatever the individual chooses, which in itself is entirely without value. What I choose to do with my freedom could be wholly destructive to myself as well as to others. For freedom to be worth anything we have to have notions about what it is good to choose. But once we see that, the tension with community disappears. Freedom is for the common good.

However, in order to sustain such a notion of freedom as rooted in givenness and dependence, and fulfilling itself in serving the common good, we need a good deal more than this notion of freedom itself. We need a context of other beliefs and values. This is only possible when the hyper-individualistic, modern or postmodern person is able to transcend their supposedly autonomous, self-sufficient, wholly self-determining selves, and find their true selves in relation to the truly determinative reality that graciously gives them selves that subsist in freedom and relationships.[4]

4. I have explored the concept of freedom at greater length in Richard Bauckham, *God and the Crisis of Freedom: Biblical and Contemporary Perspectives* (Louisville: Westminster John Knox, 2002).

CHAPTER 6

Humans, Animals, and the Environment in Genesis 1–3

1. Creation in Seven Days (Genesis 1:1–2:4a)

The account of creation in seven days (Gen 1:1–2:4a) is not the only creation account in the Bible. As well as Genesis 2:4b-25, generally recognized as a second creation account, there are at least four others (Job 38:4-11; Ps. 104:2b-9; Prov. 8:22-31; John 1:1-5). But the canonical placing of the seven-day account at the beginning of the Torah and the beginning of Scripture does give it an eminent role as foundational for the rest of the scriptural narrative. It is not surprising that it has had much the greatest influence on Christian understanding of the relationship between humanity and the nonhuman creation. In my view, it has had too exclusive an influence, and in the context of our age of ecological catastrophe, the perspectives of other parts of Scripture urgently need also to be appropriated,[1] but they lie outside my present task.

Structure and Meaning

The passage is carefully and intricately structured, and much of the meaning is embodied in the structure. The following diagram explicates the most important elements in the structure of the six days narrative:

---

1. See Richard Bauckham, *Bible and Ecology: Rediscovering the Community of Creation* (London: Darton, Longman & Todd; Waco, Tex.: Baylor University Press, 2010).

Environments + Names	Inhabitants + Tasks
[pre-creation: earth, waters, darkness: formless and unproductive]	
(Day 1) light — separated from darkness *God saw that it was good* God names: Day and Night	(Day 4) heavenly lights Task: to separate day from night, to give light, to rule *God saw that it was good*
(Day 2) firmament — separates waters God names: Sky	(Day 5) Water produces water creatures Birds in sky *God saw that it was good* God blesses Task: to be fruitful and fill
(Day 3) dry land — by gathering waters God names: Land and Sea *God saw that it was good* Land produces vegetation *God saw that it was good*	(Day 6) Land produces land creatures *God saw that it was good* Humans in God's image God blesses Task: to be fruitful and fill and subdue Dominion over creatures of (5) and (6) All creatures of (5) and (6) to live from vegetation of (3) *God saw all that he had made and it was very good*

Despite the use of a scheme of days, the allocation of material to the days follows primarily a spatial rather than a chronological arrangement. On the first three days God creates the three environments that constitute the ordered space of creation, and then, on the fourth, fifth, and sixth days, he creates the inhabitants of each of these cosmic habitats in turn. Each of the habitats is named by God, and two of them (the waters and the land) participate in the creation of their inhabitants. Vegetation is treated as an aspect of the third environment, rather than as inhabitants of it, because it is viewed as part of the land's provision for the living creatures that inhabit it. The inhabitants are all animate creatures, including the heavenly bodies (seen as animate at least because of their regular and autonomous movement). Whereas God names the environments, he gives to each category of inhabitants (with the exception of the nonhuman land creatures)[2] a task that relates both to their specific environment and to the continuance of the created order in the future. In the cases of the creatures of sea and air and of humans the task is given along with God's blessing because it is this that enables them to procreate and multiply, sharing to that extent in God's creative work.

The scheme is primarily spatial. There is also a degree of logical sequence: the work of the third day has to follow that of the second, and the environments have to be created before their respective inhabitants. What is lacking, however, is any sense of building toward a culmination. Humans, the last creatures to be created, have a unique role within creation, but they do not come last because they are the climax of an ascending scale. The "creeping things" (reptiles and insects), created on the sixth day, are not higher, in some order of being, than the birds, created on the fifth day. So this scheme of creation has nothing in common with that progressivist reading of evolution that envisages a process of increasing complexity and increasing intelligence that culminates in human beings.

If the scheme is primarily spatial rather than chronological, we may wonder why it is set in a framework of seven days. One function of the temporal framework is to convey that, along with creating a spatially ordered creation, God created a temporal structure for that creation (the perpetuation of which is entrusted to the heavenly lights). But the fact that the number seven symbolizes completeness (not unconnected with the fact that a week has seven days) is also important. As well as the sequence of seven days, the micro-structure of the account is replete with series of sevens, of which the most important is the sevenfold occurrence of the word *bara'* ("to create").[3] That God completed his whole work of creation in the six days is emphasized in the account of the seventh day, on which he rested, presumably with the implication that he rested in appreciation of all

---

2. The reason for this omission is unclear, but that these creatures also have the task of procreating and multiplying seems to be assumed.

3. William P. Brown, *The Ethos of the Cosmos: The Genesis of Moral Imagination in the Bible* (Grand Rapids: Eerdmans, 1999), p. 52.

that he had brought into being. The seventh day (rather than the creation of humans) is the true culmination of the work of creation, but not in the sense of ending a series that moves progressively toward it. Rather the seventh day, radically different in kind from the others, relates directly to each of the six and forms the vantage point from which the work of all six days may be seen, not as a sequence but as a whole.

God's approbation and appreciation of every part of his creation are conveyed by the refrain, repeated at each stage of creation: "God saw that it was good." This indicates that each part of creation has its own value that does not depend for its value on other parts. The environments, for example, are not valued only because they serve as environments for their inhabitants. While the account stresses the importance of vegetation as food for the land animals, it does not require us to think that this is its only value. God appreciates the trees and plants also for their own sake. Nevertheless, the creation was designed to be an interconnecting and interdependent whole, and so the refrain is varied at the end of the work of the sixth day: "God saw everything that he had made, and, behold, it was very good" (1:31).[4] The value of the whole is more than the value of the sum of its parts.

The general picture of creation conveyed by the account features order, diversity, and profusion of life.

The Human Place in Creation

Humans, with their unique role in creation (to which we shall turn shortly), are essential to the design of the whole, but so are the other parts of creation. The view, which was common in much of the Christian tradition, that the rest of creation was created for the sake of humans, finds no support in the text. But there are three features of the account, prior to the creation of humans, that show it to be written from the point of view of the human place in creation: (1) The heavenly lights are created "to separate the day from the night" and to "be for signs and for seasons and for days and years" (1:14). Though the distinguishing of light and darkness, day and night, benefits all creatures (see Ps. 104:20-22), the calendrical use of the movements of the heavenly bodies, implied by the second set of functions, is peculiarly human.

---

4. There are six occurrences of "God saw that it was good," and this distinctive variation is therefore the climactic seventh.

(2) In the account of the creation of the land animals "cattle" *(behe-mah)* are distinguished from "wild animals of the land" (1:24, 25, 26). Usually when such a distinction is made, the "cattle" are domesticated animals, such as oxen, sheep and goats. The account evidently sees such animals as already, at their creation, intended to share their lives with humans. Since this whole account of creation depicts humans and animals as vegetarians (1:29-30), killing domestic animals for food is not envisaged here; their roles as beasts of burden and as supplying wool and perhaps milk must be in view. Domestic animals were so integral to the life of ancient Israel that humans could hardly be envisaged without such animals nor such animals apart from humans (note their inclusion in the Sabbath law [Exod. 20:10] and even in national repentance [Jon. 3:7-8]). It is not, however, implied that such animals were created solely for the sake of humans, and it could well be that the relationship between humans and domestic animals was seen as one of mutual benefit (Psalm 23 presupposes that sheep benefit from having a shepherd).[5]

(3) At the creation of vegetation, it is described as "plants bearing seed, and fruit trees of every kind on earth that bear fruit with the seed in it" (1:11). Almost all of this rather cumbersome description is repeated in the following verse, and again when God grants humans their food supply: "I have given you every plant yielding seed that is upon the face of all the earth, and every tree with seed in its fruit" (1:29). By contrast, the food given to the land animals is described merely as "every green plant" (1:30). As Ellen Davis has recently argued, the full description, which insists so emphatically on seeds, alludes to agriculture, a uniquely human practice.[6] Again, this does not mean that seed-bearing plants and fruit trees were created solely so that humans could cultivate them, but it does mean that the creation of plants is viewed in the account from the perspective especially of humans dependent on agriculture for food.

Humans are one of two categories of creatures to whom God gives the special task of "ruling": the sun and the moon "rule" *(mashal)* the day and the night (1:16-18), while humans "rule" *(radah)* all the creatures that inhabit sea, air, and land (1:26, 28). The latter are created in "the image of

5. From the perspective of modern knowledge, we may note that domestication evidently took place in processes by which the animals attached themselves to human society, rather than being forcibly enslaved by humans: see Stephen Budiansky, *The Covenant of the Wild: Why Animals Chose Domestication* (London: Weidenfeld & Nicolson, 1994).

6. Ellen F. Davis, *Scripture, Culture, and Agriculture: An Agrarian Reading of the Bible* (Cambridge: Cambridge University Press, 2009), pp. 48-51.

God" presumably, whatever more precisely the phrase may mean, because this is what makes it possible or appropriate for them to rule over other living creatures. But we need to look quite closely at the way the human dominion is introduced and described in the two divine speeches:

> Let us make humankind in our image, according to our likeness, and **let them have dominion** [*radah*] **over the fish of the sea, and over the birds of the air, and over the cattle, and over all the wild animals**[7] **of the land, and over every creeping thing that creeps upon the land.** (1:26)

> Be fruitful and multiply, and fill the land and subdue [*kabash*] it, and **have dominion** [*radah*] **over the fish of the sea and over the birds of the air and over every living thing that moves upon the land.** (1:28)

The dominion is described in the portions of the text printed in bold type. Despite much confusion by exegetes,[8] the words that begin the second quotation are not part of the mandate of dominion. They correspond rather to what God has said to the sea creatures and the birds:

> Be fruitful and multiply and fill the waters in the seas, and let birds multiply on the land. (1:22)

The only difference is that humans are told to "subdue" *(kabash)* the land. When this verb is used with humans as its object, as it mostly is in the Old Testament, the meaning seems to be something like "to take by force" or "to make subject" (e.g., 2 Sam. 8:11; Esth. 7:8; Jer. 34:11), but when "land" *('eretz)* is the object the meaning seems more like "to occupy" or "to take possession" (Num. 32:22, 29; Josh. 18:1; 1 Chron. 22:18). This action, in

---

7. "The wild animals" does not occur in MT, LXX, or Vulgate, and therefore not in English versions until recently. NRSV, JB, REB, and NIV margin supply it from the Syriac. This correction of the MT seems very likely to be right, since "all the land/earth" in the middle of a list that is otherwise of animals is odd, and out of line with the similar lists in vv. 24, 25, and 28 (of which vv. 24-25 specifically mention "the wild animals"). The correction is accepted by Claus Westermann, *Genesis 1–11*, trans. John J. Scullion (London: SPCK, 1974), p. 79 n. 26b, although his translation (p. 77) unaccountably omits the whole of v. 26 after "image."

8. The confusion must be largely due to the text of v. 26 in MT, LXX, and Vulgate: see previous note.

these cases, requires defeating the enemies who previously occupied the land, but the land itself has only to be possessed.

In Genesis 1:28 the "land" that is to be "subdued" is the same "land" that is to be "filled" by humans (i.e., all the land in the world), and the two actions are closely connected. It seems likely that "subduing" the land here refers to agriculture, since the only way humans are able to fill the land is to cultivate it and so to make it yield more food than it would of its own accord. If the element of force is intrinsic to the verb *kabash,* then the reference is to the fact that farmers must work the land to make it yield crops.[9]

Agriculture makes the difference between fish and birds, on the one hand, and people, on the other. Without agriculture the land does not produce enough food for humans to fill it. This point must have been obvious to the biblical writers and accounts for the emphasis we have already noted on plants as seed-bearing and therefore suitable for human cultivation. Since God's command to humans is not only that they should multiply, but that they should do so to the extent of filling the land, they must also "subdue" the land, that is, farm it. Other land animals, confined to habitats that supply their food without needing to be farmed, cannot fill the land. (As well as farming, it is possible that "subduing" the land alludes also to mining metals and quarrying stone; see Deut 8:7-10.)

Of course, the command to "fill the land" should not be taken over-literally. The biblical writers were aware that there were some areas of wilderness in which humans could not live. But a more serious issue is that the creation account clearly assigns the land also to all the land animals. So God can hardly intend humans to "fill the land" at the expense of other animals. This is why, rather oddly, God's grant of "every green plant" to the land animals for food (1:30) is not spoken to the animals themselves, but appended, as information for humans, to his grant to them of seed-bearing plants for food (1:29). The point must be that humans should not grow food for themselves (and so fill the land) to an extent that competes with the livelihood of other living creatures. Humans and other creatures are to share the land, and humans are responsible for seeing that their own use of the land does not negate this sharing. There is a trace of this concern

9. Brown, *Ethos,* p. 46, speaks of "an ethos of order that requires effort but no weaponry." On the other hand, Norman Habel, "Geophany: The Earth Story in Genesis 1," in *The Earth Story in Genesis,* ed. Norman C. Habel and Shirley Wurst, Earth Bible 2 (Sheffield: Sheffield Academic, 2000), pp. 34-48, here p. 46, thinks of "harsh control."

in Israelite land law, when the people are required to leave the land fallow every seventh year "so that the poor of your people may eat; and what they leave the wild animals may eat" (Exod. 23:11; cf. Lev. 25:7). Agriculture that is too efficient deprives not only the poor but also the wild animals. (In our contemporary context we may compare the drastic decline of wildlife as a result of industrial farming methods.)

For the mandate to fill the land and subdue it we may appropriately use the term *stewardship,* since it is a right to responsible use of the land that belongs ultimately to God. But (contra most exegetes) in Genesis this is to be distinguished from the dominion over other living creatures. There is, implicitly, a connection between the two. The uniquely human practice of agriculture enables humans to multiply and spread so that they become the dominant species on earth. (Even in the Old Testament period this must have seemed to be the case.) But the dominion granted by God presupposes more than this fact of power. It also presupposes that humans bear the divine image, so that God can authorize them to use their superior power in a way that reflects God's own rule over his creation. Whereas they are to "subdue" the earth, they are to "rule" *(radah)* the other living creatures.[10]

Unlike *kabash,* which is elsewhere used of land as well as people, *radah* is used, outside Genesis 1, almost exclusively with human individuals or groups as its object. (The only exception is the problematic Joel 4:13 [3:13], where the word may be from a different root.)[11] It is not surprising that, since it refers to rule or supremacy, it is often associated with violence or force, but this does not mean that violence or force is integral to the meaning of the word. In Ezekiel 34:4 it is used of the shepherds of the flock (representing rulers of the people) who are accused of not caring for the sheep but instead ruling *(radah)* them "with force and harshness." The implication is probably that they should have ruled *(radah)* with care and compassion, as God, the true shepherd of his people, does.

10. Psalm 8:6 does not speak of a more extensive dominion. The "all" of this verse comprises the creatures specified in the following two verses. Inanimate nature is not in view.

11. Norbert Lohfink, *Theology of the Pentateuch: Themes of the Priestly Narrative and Deuteronomy,* trans. Linda M. Malony (Edinburgh: T&T Clark, 1994), pp. 11-12. But Lohfink's suggestion that the dominion refers to the domestication of animals is implausible because 1:26, as well as referring to birds and sea creatures, distinguishes "wild animals" from "cattle" (domestic animals).

It is not clear whether the dominion over other living creatures includes the right to use them in any way. In the context of Genesis 1, there is no question of killing them for food: both humans and animals are vegetarian. Other uses of animals — as beasts of burden, for wool or milk — can apply only to the domestic animals, and so could constitute only a minor part of what dominion over all living creatures — in the sea, in the air, and on the land — could mean. It seems better to exclude use of animals from the meaning of dominion. The human dominion, like God's, is a matter not of use but of care. Genesis itself provides us with a paradigm case: Noah's preservation of the animals during the flood.[12]

It is therefore significant and intelligible that the image of God is connected not with the subduing of the earth but with the dominion over other living creatures. When humans obey the command to be fruitful and multiply, to fill the earth and subdue it, they are not imitating God in a unique way but behaving like other species. All species use their environment and, though agriculture is unique to humans, it can be seen as a peculiarly human extension of the right of all animals to use their environment in order to live and to flourish. If the human dominion over other creatures were merely a matter of power, it too would be only the superlative version of what other creatures have. What links it to the image of God is that it is a delegated participation in God's caring rule over his creatures.

The fact that humans are commanded to do what other species do as well as, uniquely, to exercise dominion over other species is important to our understanding of the latter. Creation in the image of God does not make them demigods. They are unequivocally creatures. They are land animals who must live from the land as all land animals must. They participate in the ordered interdependence of the creatures as Genesis 1 portrays them. The dominion God gives them is over fellow creatures, and it reflects God's rule in a necessarily creaturely way. It is to be exercised within the created order that God has established and must serve that order.

The dominion is over living creatures, not inanimate nature. This makes the verb *radah,* which elsewhere has only humans as its object, appropriate. Unlike the sun and the moon who rule only the day and the night, humans rule other sentient beings, who are to some degree subjects of their own lives just as humans are. Genesis does distinguish quite

---

12. Odil Hannes Steck, *World and Environment,* Biblical Encounters (Nashville: Abingdon, 1980), p. 106.

sharply between living creatures and the rest of creation. The covenant of Genesis 9 is made by God with Noah and his descendants and "with every living creature that is with you, the birds, the domestic animals, and every animal of the earth with you, as many as came out of the ark" (9:9-10). It is assumed that, unlike trees and mountains, animate creatures are suitable partners in a covenant (see also Hos. 2:18). (Our modern use of the term "the environment" — as a single term embracing landscape, flora, and fauna — thus fits the perspective of Genesis very badly.)

Genesis 1 as Ecotopia[13]

As has often been observed, by contrast with other ancient creation myths, God in Genesis 1 does not battle or struggle with forces of chaos in order to wrest order from or impose order on them. God simply commands ordered form to appear out of the formless disorder of the precreation state (which in Gen. 1:2 is a kind of vividly imagined nothingness). There is no hint of a continuing threat to order from chaos. The whole process of creation proceeds in uninterrupted order, and within creation there is differentiated harmony with no hint of conflict. Crucially, neither humans nor other animals are carnivorous. So the human dominion over other living creatures involves no conflict. Its exercise ensures that there is no competition for living space or resources. All is peaceable.

This relates to the fact that everything is also finished. As we have noticed, not only the content but also the structure of the account indicates completion. The living creatures still have to multiply and to fill their environments. But this is no more than the fulfillment of the plan and potential already in place. There is no suggestion that anything could go wrong. This cosmos seems to be open neither to evil nor, in consequence, to redemption.

With a modern knowledge of the history of life on earth, we have to say: It was never like that. But the way the biblical narrative itself continues is in considerable tension with this picture of a creation already completed in the beginning. Things can go wrong and very soon do. In the light of the whole biblical narrative, the finished character of creation in Genesis 1 takes on a proleptic character, anticipating the new creation with which

13. I borrow the term from Bill Devall, *Simple in Means, Deep in Ends: Practising Deep Ecology* (London: Green Print, 1990), p. 34 ("ecotopian visions").

the narrative ends in Revelation 21–22. Only then will creation, rescued from corruption, enter into God's rest (Heb. 4:1-11).

Wolfhart Pannenberg comments:

> Only in the light of the eschatological consummation is the verdict justified that in the first creation story the Creator pronounced at the end of the sixth day when he had created the first human pair: "And God saw everything that he had made, and behold, it was very good" (Gen. 1:31). Only in the light of the eschatological consummation may this be said of our world as it is in all its confusion and pain. But those who may say it in spite of the suffering of the world honor and praise God as their Creator. The verdict "very good" does not apply simply to the world of creation in its state at any given time. It is true, rather, of the whole course of history in which God is present with his creatures in incursions of love that will finally lead it through the hazards and suffering of finitude to participation in his glory.[14]

Thus, in the light of the eschatological consummation, the human dominion, as Genesis 1 envisages it, becomes the hope for the peaceable kingdom depicted in Isaiah (11:1-9; 65:25), in which, under the rule of the Messiah, the wild animals will live harmoniously with the domestic animals, the carnivorous will become herbivorous, and the most vulnerable of humans, the small child, may play without danger from the once deadly creeping things. This is an ecotopia that is both impossible to realize short of the new creation but also an invitation to practice nonviolent, caring dominion to whatever extent might be possible in the meantime. It is notable that the invitation is accepted, if only in a small way, in Israel's land law (Exod. 23:11; Lev. 25:7). As I have argued elsewhere, Mark 1:13 takes up the hope of the messianic ecotopia of Isaiah 11, seeing it as proleptically established by Jesus in his peaceable companionship with wild animals in the wilderness.[15]

14. Wolfhart Pannenberg, *Systematic Theology,* trans. Geoffrey W. Bromiley (Grand Rapids: Eerdmans, 1998), 3:645.

15. Richard Bauckham, "Jesus and the Wild Animals (Mark 1:13): A Christological Image for an Ecological Age," in *Jesus of Nazareth: Lord and Christ: Essays on the Historical Jesus and New Testament Christology,* ed. Joel B. Green and Max Turner, Festschrift for I. Howard Marshall (Grand Rapids: Eerdmans, 1994), pp. 3-21, reprinted in Richard Bauckham, *Living with Other Creatures: Green Exegesis and Theology* (Waco, Tex.: Baylor University Press, 2011; Milton Keynes: Paternoster Press, 2012), pp. 111-32.

Contemporary Comment

The order of the cosmos portrayed in Genesis has been unprecedentedly disrupted by modern humanity's scientific-technological project of unlimited domination of the whole world. Modern humans have overfilled the earth and grossly depleted its resources without regard to the fate of other species. Genesis 1 coheres closely with the lesson taught over and over by ecological catastrophe, already happening or unavoidably imminent: that humans must exercise their right to put the earth to use within strict ecological limits and that they exceed these limits at their own peril, as well as that of other species and the planet itself. Our modern knowledge of the interconnectedness of all life on earth can provide us with renewed appreciation of the Genesis 1 creation account's portrayal of the ordered interrelationships of the creatures, while its emphasis on variety warrants contemporary concerns about biodiversity.

Genesis 1 does not authorize an undifferentiated human rule over the rest of creation, even when this is interpreted as stewardship. It distinguishes between human use of the earth, with its vegetation, for human life and flourishing, a right to be exercised responsibly, and human dominion over the rest of the animate creation, for which humans have a responsibility of care. Because of the interrelationships of all creatures, these two aspects of the human place in creation do tend to converge, especially in the face of ecological catastrophe, but the distinction remains important. Neglect of this distinction and the classification of sentient creatures as simply part of the "environment" have led to all manner of cruelty to animals. Its most contemporary manifestation is the bioengineering of animals, which presupposes that humans have as much right to redesign the animal creation for their own use as they have to plant gardens and build houses.

2. In and Out of the Garden (Genesis 2:4b–3:24)

This so-called second creation narrative doubtless originated independently of Genesis 1:1–2:4a, but in the composition of the book of Genesis it is presented not as an alternative to Genesis 1:1–2:4a but as a more detailed treatment of human origins, supplementing what Genesis 1:26-29 says on that subject.[16] I shall treat it in that way here. By comparison with

16. Cf., e.g., Bernard F. Batto, *Slaying the Dragon: Mythmaking in the Biblical Tradi-*

Genesis 1:1–2:4a, it adopts a more exclusively anthropocentric perspective. The animals, for example, are considered only from the point of view of whether they could provide the "helper" Adam needs (2:18-20). The story itself might appear to present this as the sole reason for their creation, but were this really the case their creation would have been a mistake, since all of them fail to qualify for the role in question. But the story is a way of explicating the relationship between Adam and the animals: by naming them, he recognizes them as fellow creatures with whom he shares the world,[17] but his relationship with them is of a different order from his relationship with another human being, "flesh of his flesh."

Whereas the seven-days' creation account ensures the creatureliness of humans by placing them within the order of creation, the Eden account does so, perhaps more emphatically, by stressing Adam's kinship with the earth and the other creatures of earth. God, we are told, "formed the human being ['*adam*] from the dust of the soil ['*adamah*]"[18] (2:7) — the pun draws attention to the relationship and indicates its appropriateness. The animals are also created from the soil, all them individually molded, like Adam, by God (2:19). God animates the clay figure of Adam by breathing into him "the breath of life" (2:7), which is the same breath that animates all living creatures (7:22). Though not specifically mentioned in the account of the creation of the animals (2:19), it must be assumed, because otherwise the animals would not be alive. The summary account probably assumes that, just as God himself formed both Adam and the animals from the soil, so God himself breathed the breath of life into both Adam and the animals. The phrase "living being" *(nefesh hayyah),* used of Adam in 2:7,

---

tion (Louisville: Westminster John Knox, 1992), p. 99: The priestly editor "did not consider having two different stories of the same 'event' to be contradictory or problematic. Instead, he likely regarded them as complementary."

17. The naming is not a matter of asserting his authority over them, as has often been suggested. If it were, then the same would have to be said of his naming of Eve (2:23; 3:20). Rather Adam's naming of the animals is comparable with the naming of children by parents (usually, in the Old Testament, the mother), which does not assert authority but recognizes the independent reality of a new person. See George W. Ramsey, "Is Name-Giving an Act of Domination in Genesis 2:23 and Elsewhere?," *Catholic Biblical Quarterly* 50 (1988): 24-35. According to Mark G. Brett, "Earthing the Human in Genesis 1–3," in Habel and Wurst, *Earth Story in Genesis,* pp. 73-86, here p. 81, the naming is "a celebration of diversity." I see no basis for Brown's claim (*Ethos,* p. 141) that Adam determines the roles of the animals.

18. For '*adamah* as "arable land, fertile soil that can be cultivated," see Theodore Hiebert, *The Yahwist's Landscape: Nature and Religion in Early Israel* (Oxford: Oxford University Press, 1996), pp. 34-35.

elsewhere always refers to animals. Nothing in their created constitution differentiates humans from other animals.

Moreover, Adam's life remains bound up with the soil. Before we hear of him, we hear of the soil's need of him: "there was no one to till ['avad] the ground ['adamah]" (2:5). Once created, Adam is placed by God in the garden he has planted "to till ['avad] it and keep [shamar] it" (2:15). Following the description of the rivers of Eden (2:10-14), which associate it with Mesopotamia,[19] where the rivers themselves were not sufficient to make most of the land fertile, Adam's task is probably to irrigate the land in order to sustain the trees God has planted there.[20] Later he is sent to perform the same task outside Eden: "to till the ground from which he was taken" (3:23).[21] The man from the soil must work the soil in order to live from the soil's produce. The task is probably, as we have seen, much the same as that intended by the command to "subdue the land" in Genesis 1:28, but here there is a stronger sense of humanity's close relationship with the soil. It seems to be a reciprocal relationship: the soil needs Adam's work and he needs the soil's produce. There is also, in the word "keep" or "preserve," the implication that Adam takes care of the soil. He avoids exhausting it. (Several recent studies of the passage have proposed translating 'avad as "to serve," either as the sole meaning or as an additional overtone.[22] But, whereas this verb with a personal object means "to serve," there is a consistent usage of the verb to mean "to work" or "to cultivate" when the object is inanimate [Gen 3:23; 4:12; Deut 28:39; Isa 19:9; cf. Prov 12:11; 28:19; Zech 13:5]. This is the obvious meaning in Genesis 2.)[23]

---

19. I say "associate it with," rather than "locate it in" Mesopotamia, because it may be that the geography is intentionally obscure, suggesting that Eden cannot be geographically located in the ordinary sense (Batto, *Slaying,* p. 49).

20. Brown, *Ethos,* p. 139.

21. According to Ronald A. Simkins, *Creator and Creation: Nature in the Worldview of Ancient Israel* (Peabody, Mass.: Hendrickson, 1994), p. 180, humans are placed only temporarily in the garden, until they reach maturity and can be sent out to farm the land elsewhere.

22. E.g. Hiebert, *Yahwist's Landscape,* p. 157; Steven Bouma-Prediger, *For the Beauty of the Earth: A Christian Vision for Creation Care* (Grand Rapids: Baker Academic, 2001), p. 74; Norman Wirzba, *The Paradise of God: Renewing Religion in an Ecological Age* (Oxford: Oxford University Press, 2003), p. 31; Norman Habel, *An Inconvenient Text: Is a Green Reading of the Bible Possible?* (Adelaide: ATF Press, 2009), p. 69.

23. Davis, *Scripture,* pp. 29-30, tries to have her cake and eat it when translating both 'avad and shamar: "to work and serve it, to preserve and observe it." But this seems to be an instance of the fallacy of attributing to a word in one occurrence the sum of the various meanings it carries in a number of other occurrences.

The Old Testament often supposes a triangular relationship between God, humans, and the earth. Disruption of humanity's relationship with God affects also their relationship with the earth.[24] This is what happens in Genesis 3, when, following the primal act of disobedience to God, the ground is cursed and an element of hostility and resistance spoils the hitherto harmonious reciprocity of Adam's relationship to it (3:17-19).

Contemporary Comment

The modern project of scientific-technological domination of nature has been characterized by the desire to transcend nature, escaping from its constraints and remaking it to our own design. This is in effect a desire to be like God, with unlimited power and the freedom to create as we choose. The transfer of divine attributes from God to humans, perceived as occupying the place of God in relation to the world, not in creation but above it, is explicit in the Renaissance humanists[25] and formed much of the ethos of the modern world. It is, of course, the temptation to which Adam and Eve succumbed. In the Genesis narrative, Adam and Eve eat the fruit that the serpent tells them will make them like God, but they remain creatures, bound up with the earth, dependent on it, and destined to return to it. Similarly, the modern project has left us once again creatures. The attempt to transcend nature, to re-create it as we would like it to be, has brought upon us the ecological disasters that are its unforeseen consequences. We are obliged now to recognize the extent to which we must respect the limits of our finite place in the ecological balance of the planet.

The modern attempt to transcend all limits was based, in the Renaissance humanists, on an interpretation of the divine image of Genesis 1:26-27. Though this neglected the limiting context within which Genesis 1 places humans, the account of humanity in Genesis 1 certainly offers more pretext for a notion of human transcendence of creation than the account in Genesis 2 does. In that sense, Genesis 2, with its stress on humanity's belonging to the earth and among the creatures of the earth, should help to bring us down to earth again.

24. Robert Murray, *The Cosmic Covenant,* Heythrop Monographs 7 (London: Sheed & Ward, 1992), chaps. 2 and 4.

25. Richard Bauckham, *God and the Crisis of Freedom: Biblical and Contemporary Perspectives* (Louisville: Westminster John Knox, 2002), pp. 154-59.

The necessary human connection with the soil easily escapes the attention of modern urban people whose lives seem to be sustained by technology rather than by the produce of the land. The sumptuous availability of the latter in the affluent West means that we do not have to think much about their source, though uneasiness with the artificiality of modern farming methods has led to some such thinking and to the movement back to organic food. But in the face of the looming world shortage of food, likely to be disastrously intensified by climate change, a movement back to a degree of local self-sufficiency, entailing urban people's reconnection with the soil, begins to seem desirable. At the same time old-fashioned care for the soil begins to seem wiser than industrial-scale exploitation. We do not live in Eden, but even outside Eden something of Adam's symbiotic relationship with the soil, depending on it and caring for it, remains available.

CHAPTER 7

The Story of the Earth according to Paul

Romans 8:19-23 has been described as "an environmental mantra,"[1] meaning that appeal is often made to it as a kind of ecological prooftext, mandating environmental activity by Christians, without engaging in exegetical detail with the problems of interpreting the passage. We cannot here solve all the exegetical problems, but we shall attempt to elucidate the way in which Paul here situates the plight of the nonhuman creation within the biblical metanarrative.[2] While this may not exactly mandate environmental activity by contemporary Christians, it may be able to give us much-needed orientation within the multiple ecological crises that we unavoidably face today.

Romans 8:18-23

I consider that the sufferings of this present time are not worth comparing with the glory about to be revealed to us. 19For the creation waits with eager longing for the revealing of the children of God; 20for

---

1. Cherryl Hunt, David G. Horrell, and Christopher Southgate, "An Environmental Mantra? Ecological Interest in Romans 8:19-23 and a Modest Proposal for Its Narrative Interpretation," *Journal of Theological Studies* 59 (2008): 546-79.

2. I am especially indebted to the following studies: Laurie J. Braaten, "All Creation Groans: Romans 8:22 in Light of the Biblical Sources," *Horizons in Biblical Theology* 28 (2006): 131-59; Jonathan Moo, "Romans 8.19-22 and Isaiah's Cosmic Covenant," *New Testament Studies* 54 (2008): 74-89; Hunt, Horrell, and Southgate, "An Environmental Mantra?" 546-79; Brendan Byrne, "An Ecological Reading of Rom. 8:19-22: Possibilities and Hesitations," in *Ecological Hermeneutics: Biblical, Historical and Theological Perspectives,* ed. David G. Horrell, Cherryl Hunt, Christopher Southgate, and Francesca Stavrakopoulou (London: T&T Clark, 2010), pp. 83-93.

the creation was subjected to futility, not of its own will but by the will of the one who subjected it, in hope 21that the creation itself will be set free from its bondage to decay and will obtain the freedom of the glory of the children of God. 22We know that the whole creation has been groaning and in travail together until now; 23and not only the creation, but we ourselves, who have the first fruits of the Spirit, groan inwardly while we wait for adoption, the redemption of our bodies.[3]

Much recent writing on biblical hermeneutics has familiarized us with the notion (obvious once it is pointed out) that the Bible's message primarily takes narrative form. The Bible tells the grand narrative, or metanarrative, of God's dealings with his world from creation in the beginning, through sin and salvation, to the renewal or perfecting of all creation at the end. Paul in Romans is engaged in formulating, explaining, and defending his own version of this narrative. In Paul's telling it is a narrative of God, Jesus, Israel, and the nations. But he does not entirely neglect the fact that in the Hebrew Bible, there is another key character in the grand narrative: the nonhuman creation. One reason Paul does not neglect it is that he never downplays the material aspect of human nature and envisages salvation as entailing, not redemption from the body, but the redemption of the body, the renewal and perfecting of humans precisely in their full bodily integrity. It is no accident, then, that our passage ends with the future hope of believers characterized as "the redemption of our bodies" (v. 23). Human bodies are our solidarity with the rest of this material creation, and this solidarity makes it appropriate that the bodily redemption of believers accompanies the renewal of the whole created world. Because Paul's focus in Romans 8 is on the relationship of present suffering and hope for the future, he devotes this short passage to putting believers' experience of suffering and hope within the larger context of the suffering and hope of the whole creation. Between believers and the nonhuman creatures there is a solidarity not only of material constitution but also of "groaning" and hope for future liberation and glory.

3. The translation is from the NRSV, except that in v. 22 I have substituted "groaning and in travail together" for the NRSV's "groaning in labor pains." In the Greek there are two verbs *(systenazei* and *synōdinei),* both with the prefix *syn* (meaning "together" and most likely suggesting that the nonhuman creation groans and suffers judgment along with humans). The "groaning" is probably not the cries of a woman in labor but a distinct reference to the mourning of creation, while "in travail" does not imply a positive outcome, but simply being the object of God's judgment (e.g., Jer. 4:31; 1 Thess. 5:3).

The biblical narrative is a story with three essential "characters": God, humans, and the nonhuman creation. (If we read the narrative in a trinitarian perspective, then all three "characters" comprise a multiplicity of subjects. In the case of the third we should not let the summarizing term "creation" or "nonhuman creation" obscure the fact that it includes a vast plurality and enormous diversity of creatures.) In the modern period the biblical narrative has all too often been represented as a story about God and humans. The rest of creation could be forgotten because it was thought of as a mere stage-set for the human drama or merely a resource for humans to exploit in the interests of the human story. It ceased to be an active character. It has taken our contemporary awareness of the catastrophic disruption of the relationship between humans and other creatures to reawaken us to the fact that our history is a history of mutual interdependence and reciprocal interaction between humans, the earth, and the other creatures with whom we share the earth. We can thereby appreciate afresh the fact that the biblical story is of a three-way relationship. Just as humans are related to God and also to the nonhuman creation, so the nonhuman creation has its own relationship to God as well as its relationship to humans. In the biblical narrative it is quite clear that the human "dominion" over other living creatures (Gen 1:26, 28) does not mean that all relationship between God and the nonhuman creation is mediated by humans.

Our Pauline passage is a concise version of the biblical grand narrative, a version in which all three characters (God, humans, and the nonhuman creation) appear, but in which the nonhuman creation takes center stage. Creation is the subject of all the important verbs in verses 19-22: the creation waits with eager longing,[4] was subjected to futility, will be set free, has been groaning, has been in travail. God seems to be behind the scenes, concealed by the two divine passives ("was subjected" [v. 20], "will be set free" [v. 21]) and the cryptic anonymity of "the one who subjected" (v. 20: *ton hypotaxanta*).[5] God's action is certainly decisive in the story, but Paul keeps God in the background perhaps because he wishes to focus on the solidarity of the other two characters. For just as creation waits, so do believers; just as creation is to be set free, so will believers; just as creation groans, so do believers. The two are bound up together in the same story, but there is an imbalance. Creation, it appears, is the innocent victim of

---

4. In the Greek the subject of "waits" is "the eager longing of the creation."

5. It is debated whether "the one who subjected" is God, but this seems much the most likely possibility.

human wrongdoing, since "it was subjected to futility, not of its own will" (v. 20), and must therefore await the liberation of humans before it too can be liberated and participate in the coming glory (v. 21). The intimate connection between creation and humans has so far been to creation's detriment, but eventually it will be to its advantage. Meanwhile they are bound up together both in suffering and in hope.

What exactly is the plight of creation, from which it longs for deliverance? Most exegetes have seen in verse 20 ("the creation was subjected to futility") a reference to the fall of Genesis 3, where God curses the ground because of Adam's sin, with the result that farming will be harder work (Gen. 3:17). But this does not seem an adequate basis for Paul's claim that the whole creation is in "bondage to decay," "groaning and in travail" as it longs for future liberation. At most, the aorist verb in verse 20 ("was subjected") might refer to God's initial act of subjecting the creation to the abuse that will be done to it by fallen humanity. But, probably more importantly, the whole passage reflects the theme to be found on several occasions in the Prophets: that the nonhuman creation as a whole suffers the effects of human sin and God's judgment on it. Sometimes the land or the earth (*'eretz*) is said to "mourn" (Jer. 4:28; 12:4; Hos. 4:3; Joel 1:10), and it may be that Paul's reference to the creation "groaning" echoes such passages. In the Prophets the earth's "mourning" is addressed, in complaint and supplication, to God, and this is probably also true of the creation's "groaning" in Romans 8:22, especially in the light of verses 23 and 26.

The prophets use this image to portray the kind of devastation of land, through severe drought or desertification, that leaves its vegetation withering and its animal life failing. We could call it ecological death. The prophets see it as God's judgment on human sin — not the once-for-all curse of Genesis 3, but the curse that human sin brings down on the earth over and over again. Moreover, while the prophetic texts address the localized situations of Israel's history, they are also prone to use remarkably universalistic language (especially Jer. 4:23-28; Hos. 4:3) that easily suggests, in Paul's language, that "the whole creation has been groaning and in travail together until now" (v. 22). An equivalently universal version of the same prophetic theme is to be found in Isaiah 24:4-6 (and cf. Zeph. 1:2-3).

In the light of this scriptural background, we can see that, when Paul speaks of the creation's "bondage to decay" (v. 21), he is not referring to death as a universal feature of the animal and vegetable creations, understood as resulting from the sin of Adam and Eve, but to processes of ecological degradation and destruction that occur frequently and widely where humans live. Creation's "bondage to decay" is its subjection to such processes of devastation.

Among the prophetic depictions of the earth mourning, Joel's account is the most vivid and may serve to fill out Paul's rather abstract language:

> 10The fields are devastated,
>   the ground mourns;
> for the grain is destroyed,
>   the wine dries up,
>   the oil fails.
>
> 11Be dismayed, you farmers,
>   wail, you vinedressers,
> over the wheat and the barley;
>   for the crops of the field are ruined.
> 12The vine withers,
>   the fig tree droops.
> Pomegranate, palm, and apple —
>   all the trees of the field are dried up;
> surely, joy withers away
>   among the people. . . .
>
> 17The seed shrivels under the clods,
>   the storehouses are desolate;
> the granaries are ruined
>   because the grain has failed.
> 18How the animals[6] groan!
>   The herds of cattle wander about
> because there is no pasture for them;
>   even the flocks of sheep are dazed.
>
> 19To you, O LORD, I cry.
> For fire has devoured
>   the pastures of the wilderness,
> and flames have burned
>   all the trees of the field.

6. These are the domestic animals, distinguished from the wild animals in v. 20.

20Even the wild animals cry[7] to you
   because the watercourses are dried up,
and fire has devoured
   the pastures of the wilderness. (Joel 1:10-12, 17-20)

It is notable that in this passage, whereas the other prophets speak of the mourning of the earth, Joel depicts all kinds of creatures mourning, lamenting, and groaning to God: the ground (v. 10), the domestic animals (v. 18), the wild animals (v. 20), as well as the farmers (v. 11), the people (v. 12), and the prophet himself (v. 19). It is easy to see here both how Paul could generalize the mourning as that of the whole creation and how he can understand it as paralleling the "mourning" of human believers (v. 23). The desiccation and devastation of nature, also extensively depicted by Joel, are the object of the mourning, and represent, in Paul's terms, creation's subjection to futility, meaning something like "being prevented from fulfilling its purpose of flourishing and fruitfulness."

The prophets understood that the behavior of humans and the well-being of the rest of creation are intimately related both to each other and to God. This makes good sense within the threefold relationship of which the biblical metanarrative is the story. Sometimes they speak of these consequences of human evil as the direct interventions of God in judgment (e.g., Isa. 24:1-4; Zeph. 1:2-3), sometimes as though they are processes built into the order of creation as God has created it (e.g., Hos. 4:1-3). The two are not necessarily in contradiction. The prophets did not, of course, have the scientific understanding of the connections between humans and the rest of creation that modern ecology is giving us. On the whole we have become aware of such connections only as our ignoring of them has led to consequences too considerable to be ignored. But in many such cases the human activities that have led and are leading to such destructive consequences have not been pursued through pardonable ignorance or simple foolishness. They have been driven by greed or the will to power, arrogance or aggression, and not infrequently injustice and oppression in human society have gone hand in hand with ecological destruction. The natural order and the moral order are by no means unconnected.

According to Romans 8, the liberation of creation from the destructive effects of human sin is to happen at the end of history, when Christian

---

7. The rare verb *'arag* may mean "to long for," as in Ps. 42:2. Might it be the basis for *apokaradokia* ("eager expectation") in Rom. 8:19?

believers will attain their full salvation in the glory of the resurrection (vv. 21, 23). Since creation's bondage is due to human sin, its liberation must await the cessation of human evil at the end. It might seem, therefore, that this passage cannot mandate human activity for the relief of creation from the burden of human mistreatment now, in the present age. It is true that that is not Paul's concern in the passage. But if we accept the diagnosis, that human wrongdoing is responsible for ecological degradation, it follows that those who are concerned to live according to God's will for his world must be concerned to avoid and to repair damage to God's creation as far as possible. We cannot achieve the eschatological liberation of creation, but we can anticipate it. This would accord well with the way Paul in this very passage portrays believers as already participating in the life of the age to come in an anticipatory way: they have "the first fruits of the Spirit" (v. 23). This is what makes their groaning not only an expression of suffering but also a yearning in hope for the redemption yet to come. To avert and repair ecological destruction would be to *practice* the hope that believers share with the rest of creation (v. 21).

CHAPTER 8

Ecological Hope in Crisis?

Christian Hope in Our Context

The church has frequently had to think afresh about Christian hope in changing contexts. It is not that the essence of Christian hope — the great hope, founded on Jesus Christ, for God's redemptive and fulfilling renewal of all his creation — changes. But if Christian hope is to retain its power to be the engine of the church's engagement with the world, if it is to be more than an ineffective private dream, hope itself needs renewal as the world changes. From the infinite riches of God's future for the world we must draw those that can be transformative for our time. That way we can reenvision the world in the light of hope. That is what happened when John the prophet, in the book of Revelation, was taken up to heaven in order to see how the critical moment of history in which his first readers were living looked from God's perspective — from the perspective of God's purpose to actualize his kingdom on earth as it already is in heaven. John had to be abstracted in vision from the world of the beast, the world as projected by the imperial propaganda, in order, not simply to see the future goal of God's purposes, but also to see how that goal shed light on the present, how God's people there and then were to live toward the coming kingdom of God and the coming renewal of all creation. A great deal of misunderstanding of Revelation arises from missing the fact that it contextualizes the Christian hope in the realities of the late-first-century Roman Empire. It inspires and models the kind of contextualizing we need to do, but it cannot do that for us. We need, if not the revelatory vision with which John was privileged, at least the discernment of Christian wisdom to read the world aright in the light of the Christian hope and to enable us here and now to live toward the new creation.

Part of that contextualizing of Christian hope has to be engagement of some kind with the secular hopes of our time. The book of Revelation engages with Rome's pretensions to universal and eternal rule. In our own time we are still living amid the fading glory of modern progressivism, that pervasive ideology of the modern world that seduced everyone into thinking that tomorrow will — or, at least, should — be better than today. Its major surviving versions are economic neoliberalism and globalization, with their myth of never-ending economic growth, and technological optimism, with its ignorant confidence that human ingenuity will solve all our problems and put us back on track, still headed for the technological utopia in which nature will be finally mastered, all its unruly potential harnessed to our needs and desires. Both economic growth and technological optimism — natural allies, of course — are versions of the delusion that there are no limits to what we can have and do. The dawning ecological catastrophe should surely have dispelled those dreams, but such is the power of progressivism, especially in the United States, that they live on. Climate-change denial is one version of their delusive power.

Another feature of the contemporary context of Christian hope — if I may use "contemporary" to mean the last three or four decades — is that for the first time in human history humans themselves have acquired the power to annihilate human life and much of the rest of creation on this planet. Humans in the past have often faced the prospect — real or imagined — of world-destroying catastrophe. And many civilizations have collapsed through overexploitation of their natural resources, as Jared Diamond's book *Collapse* demonstrated so compellingly.[1] But only with the development of nuclear weapons capable of annihilating the human world did humans face the prospect of an entirely human-caused (anthropogenic) terminal catastrophe. In the period of the Cold War it hung like a sword of Damocles over all our lives. We have displaced that threat for the time being, though it will never go away. The ecological catastrophe that is now underway is much more complex in its causes and challenges, as well as in its foreseeable results. Moreover, while the nuclear threat, since Nagasaki and Hiroshima, has remained no more

1. Jared Diamond, *Collapse: How Societies Choose to Fail or Succeed* (London: Allen Lane, 2005; London: Penguin, 2006).

than a threat, ecological catastrophe is underway. It is engulfing us. Although, like nuclear bombs, it was created by humans, we have now, like the sorcerer's apprentice, lost control of it. It has its own momentum, which, even if humans stopped all carbon emissions worldwide tomorrow (an impossible hope), would still keep going, with some foreseeable consequences that are very alarming and doubtless others we cannot guess. If there is, for concerned Christians, a crisis of hope, I guess that is the main factor. All the books that have taught us that care of creation is a Christian responsibility, that there are all sorts of things we can do — from recycling to lobbying at climate-change summits — all seemed to assume we had time to stop anything really bad happening. They exuded hope of a fairly uncomplicated kind. Now we are realizing that, although of course we can stop things getting even worse than they will anyway, quite a lot is going wrong unstoppably. And if we haven't managed to stop what is happening — and if neither the politicians in power in China and the United States nor the Christians in the pews are taking the situation seriously — how can we go on hoping?

Ultimate Hope and Proximate Hopes

The relation between ultimate hope and proximate hopes is crucial to our topic. By ultimate hope I mean the final achievement of all God's purposes for his creation when he brings this temporal history to its end and takes the whole creation, redeemed and renewed, into his own eternal life. If we believe in the God of Jesus Christ, that is an unconditional hope that rests on God's faithfulness to his creation and the promise made in the resurrection of Jesus Christ from the dead. Christians have by no means always thought that this hope includes the nonhuman creation, but happily we have been recovering that full hope. The new heaven and the new earth are not a replacement for this creation, but its renewal, when God will take it beyond the reach of evil, death, and transience. Not only is that clear in Romans 8:19-21, for example, but also it is coherent with our own destiny as resurrection to renewed bodily life. Our bodies are our solidarity with the rest of creation. We are Adam's children, earthy, made of the stuff of this earth like the mammals, the birds, the clouds, the rivers, and all the creatures of this earth. And so is Jesus Christ, who by rising bodily from death maintained his solidarity with all the creatures of earth through death into new creation. Since new creation is a radical renewal of creation, a transposition of the created world into the conditions of eternity, our ability to conceive of it is necessarily very limited. In my view, we should think of God taking into his new creation the whole chronological extent of this creation's history, everything that has value for eternity. Extinct creatures and lost landscapes — all that God has found good in his creation — will be there. Nothing will be lost except evil and the damage it has done. Of course, we can't imagine it. Ultimate hope ought to be mind-blowing.

Proximate hopes are all the hopes we have for the temporal future. If they are fully formed Christian hopes, they, like ultimate hope, will be based on what God has done for us in Jesus Christ and on the images we are given of the goal that God is going ultimately to realize for his world. Our proximate hopes are for what we can desire and envisage that reflects, within this world, the ultimate hope of new creation. They are on the way to ultimate hope, but must always, of course, fall short of it. It is very important in our contemporary context that we distinguish this vision from modern progressivism and modern utopianism. We are not engaged in a step-by-step progress toward utopia. What we are able to do in realizing our hopes does not, as it were, accumulate, as though we were building the new Jerusalem brick by brick. Sometimes good follows good in a process of improvement; sometimes it doesn't. But the value is not dependent on progression. We have all been brainwashed by progressivism. For things to be worth doing and worth having they do not have to lead on to even better things. They have value in themselves, and nothing will be lost in the end. When Paul says that our labor will not be in vain (1 Cor. 15:58) he does not mean that it will contribute to a historical process of improvement but that it will have effects that will be preserved in the new creation.

One key difference between ultimate hope and proximate hope is that ultimate hope is unconditional. It depends only on God's transcendent act of re-creation. So Paul can call it "a hope that does not disappoint" (Rom. 5:5). But proximate hopes depend partly on what humans do. God's providence is constantly at work engaging with human evil, limiting its effects, bringing good out of it, but he does not abolish it in this world. This world will always be the ambiguous sphere in which evil can frustrate our most reasonable hopes. Proximate hopes can be disappointed. If you have been to Jerusalem, you have probably been to the modern church of Dominus Flevit on the Mount of Olives. It has a fine view over the whole of the old city of Jerusalem, and it is shaped like a tear because it commemorates Jesus' tears of disappointment, when he lamented: "Jerusalem, Jerusalem . . . How often I have desired to gather your children together, as a hen gathers her brood under her wings, but you were not willing" (Matt. 23:37). There was nothing wrong or inadequate about Jesus' hopes for the people of Jerusalem. They flowed from his love for them, which was God's love for them. His hopes were disappointed because love can be rejected.

Getting the relationship between ultimate hope and proximate hopes right has been continually problematic for Christians in the modern period. On the one hand, modern progressivism merged the two in a vision of improvement that would issue in utopia. Utopia became a goal we might achieve — with the catastrophic results we saw in Stalin's Russia and Mao's China. Utopianism is dangerous partly because it cannot content itself with what is pragmatically possible in given circumstances. It overreaches the real limits of the human situation in a massive effort to wrest history toward its utopian goals, usually involving violent suppression of dissent. When it comes to the nonhuman creation, modern utopianism was usually wedded to the technological exploitation of nature, with the sad ecological consequences we saw in the Soviet Union and Eastern Europe.

On the other hand, in the modern period traditional Christianity has been accused of the opposite error: setting its hopes on an otherworldly goal in order to keep the masses happy with their unfortunate lot here and now. Hope for another world to compensate for the ills of this one incurred the Marxist critique of being the opium of the people. I think the charge has been exaggerated, and we should not devalue the role that ultimate hope has played for people in hopeless circumstances, helping people to go on living when any hope for improvement in this world was entirely unrealistic.

But how can ultimate hope and proximate hopes relate in a way that empowers hopeful activity without falling into the trap of unrealistic utopianism? I think we need to see it like this: Ultimate hope can fund proximate hopes. It enables us to work in the direction of God's purpose, knowing that we are working with God's purpose, working with the grain of the universe. But distinguishing ultimate hope and proximate hopes enables us to be appropriately modest and realistic about what we can hope for here and now in particular contexts. We have to seek out those concrete possibilities for movement in the direction of the kingdom that we can actually identify and work with here and now. We do not hold the tiller of history. We must simply do what we can, more or less, this or that, as the case may be.

Faith, Hope, and Love

If we need to sustain, to refresh, or to renew our hope, one good approach is to reflect on the way it is connected with faith and love in that New Testament trio of Christian virtues that Paul expounds with poetic eloquence in 1 Corinthians 13. The three belong together. I am tempted to say that, like the persons of God the Trinity, they are perichoretic. In other words, they are formed through their mutual relations. Faith, hope, and love are mutually engaging, mutually sustaining, mutually enhancing, each necessary to the flourishing of the others. Among other things he says about love, Paul says that it believes all things (faith) and that it hopes all things (hope).

When Paul writes about faith, hope, and love, he is of course speaking about Christian virtues, the work of the Holy Spirit in Christian lives, but it is important to note that there are, as it were, natural versions of each. Without faith, hope, and love human beings cannot live at all. Although it may be entirely below the level of conscious reflection, all human beings live by a kind of basic trust in reality. We assume that all the ordinary things we do will have the kind of effects they usually have. Hope is natural to human beings and necessary to human life, and similarly care and concern for others, even if only a select group, are indispensable to the life of the social animals we are. In all three of these natural virtues the individual is directed outward, if not explicitly to God, at least to the world and to other humans. Sin is what impedes that positive, outward-directedness of human life, and turns people in on themselves in despair and self-centeredness.

What the Holy Spirit does is to renew and to revitalize these good aspects of what it is to be human in the world. Christian redemption is the renewal of human nature, not its replacement. What the Spirit especially does is to resource these virtues in God and to refocus them on God as their primary object. We live not by some merely implicit trust in reality, vaguely defined, but by faith in the living God. We do not just hope for the best, as they say, but place our hope in God. We love because he first loved us and by loving God we learn to love all that God loves.

The fact that these Christian virtues are the renewal of natural virtues means that it should be natural and not problematic for Christians to work with non-Christian people who care about the planet and share many of our hopes and fears for it. We have Christian distinctives, important to us, but they need not cancel out what we have in common with others.

I shall now reflect briefly on each of the three virtues and the way it relates to the others.

Love

I take this first because Paul says that love is the greatest of the three (1 Cor. 13:13). The reason may be partly that love is mutual between God and us. Preachers sometimes say that God has faith in us or that God is pinning his hopes on us. No doubt that makes a point in its own way. But Scripture does not speak that way. In the Bible God does not have faith or hope, but God does love. God loves us and we return God's love. Moreover, this is not just a closed circle. It expands as we learn to love what God loves. We come to value other people in something of the way God does, and we come to value the rest of creation in something of the way God does. This is not a case of loving only because God tells us to. It is a matter of really sharing in the movement of God's love that encompasses his whole creation and returns to him in reciprocal love. God's love for the rest of creation empowers ours.

Some time ago I was thinking about the first chapter of Genesis when I had one of those breakthrough moments when you see something significant in Scripture that you have not noticed before, even though the passage is familiar. If you read through the creation narrative in Genesis 1, you read that at the end of each day God looks at what he has created on that day and sees that it is good. In other words, he is delighted with it. He appreciates its value. I think the narrative is inviting us to share God's delight in his creation. Whenever it says, "God saw that it was good," we are prompted to agree. Knowing the created world as we do, we can enter into God's appreciation of it. So when we get to the creation of humans late on the sixth day and we read God's command to us to have dominion over the creatures, we already know that what God is entrusting to our care is something of great value. It's the world we have begun to delight in as God does. We can only exercise dominion — that is, caring responsibility for other creatures — if we have learned to appreciate them, to love them as God does.

"Love hopes all things," Paul says in 1 Corinthians 13:7. Love empowers hope. Actually, when we love, we simply cannot help hoping. No one who loves their children can fail to have hopes for them. No one who loves the lovely products of human art and culture can fail to hope that they survive to inspire others for all time. No one who loves the wild places of the world can fail to hope that they will be preserved. No one who loves red squirrels or starlings or snow leopards or rare orchids or coral reefs or tigers can fail to hope that they survive in the habitats they belong to. No one who loves and appreciates the astounding diversity of life in every nook and cranny of this diverse world can fail to hope that it can be preserved and that even the species as yet unknown to us may live for the value they have in themselves. Love inspires hope and energizes hope.

Faith

Faith is what makes Christian hope something much more than optimism about human capabilities. Faith means we do not expect to achieve what we hope for all by ourselves. It means we have to believe in providence.

Providence is a difficult doctrine, but I think essential. One way of putting it is this: God can make of what we do much more than we can make of it ourselves. What is actually happening when some human effort for the good is successful? Often it is not just a human person's act or a group of people's act that gets the result, but a collocation of unplanned circumstances that accompany the act. In other circumstances it would not have been successful. Things had to come together in just the way they did. A great deal of human achievement depends on what a secular person would have to say is just coincidence. Maybe we think too much of ourselves to think too much about that, but it doesn't undermine the importance of human achievement. What the human person is intentionally doing to get the result is essential, but it is not all that is going on. God honors what we do by making of it more than we can make of it ourselves.

An interesting biblical illustration of this is the story of the book of Esther. This a book that never mentions God. It is rather extraordinary that the Bible contains a book that never mentions God. There is one point in the text where we really cannot help thinking of God: when Mordecai says to queen Esther, "Who knows? Perhaps you have come to royal dignity for just such a time as this?" (4:14). But even here the writer scrupulously does no more than suggest that God may be at work behind the scenes. Why this curious absence of God from this narrative of a great deliverance of God's people from threatened genocide? In some ways, the story of Esther is a new exodus narrative, with Esther as the new Moses. But in the original exodus narrative God is very explicitly present — in manifest and miraculous power. Perhaps the author of Esther thought, as we are also inclined to think when we read of the pillar of fire and cloud and the parting of the Red Sea, that God doesn't seem to do that sort of thing nowadays. So is God not at work in this apparently secular world? Well, Esther does the right and rather courageous thing, and it works — but only because other events, coincidences, conspire to ensure its success. This is the anonymous work of God in a world where he is not evident in manifest interventions. He takes what Esther so resourcefully and courageously does, and he makes more of it than she could have made of it herself.

Faith is another form of protection from hubris and utopianism. What we can do is important, but we must let God make of it what he will.

Hope

"Love," says Paul, "hopes all things" (1 Cor. 13:7). Love, as we have seen, is what empowers and energizes hope, but "for all things"? Of course, this is elevated poetic style. It surely doesn't endorse indulging utterly fanciful fantasies of hope. But it raises the issue of hope and realism, which is near the heart of our concerns in the crisis of ecological hope.

The first point to make is that proximate hopes must be moderated and directed by realism about the real possibilities of the here and now. Let climate-change denial be a warning to us. People who deny climate change are devoted to the American dream of limitless economic growth. They see all the evidence for climate change as a kind of left-wing conspiracy to imperil America's great future. They refuse to face reality because they cannot surrender their very unrealistic hope.

I have learned quite a lot from Bill McKibben's most recent book, *Eaarth: Making a Life on a Tough New Planet.*[2] He spells *Eaarth* with an extra *a* in it, because, he says, we need a new name for a planet that climate change has already made a different world from the one that humans have lived in for the rest of human history. He writes to address precisely the situation that poses for us the question, How can we go

2. Bill McKibben, *Eaarth: Making a Life on a Tough New Planet,* 2nd ed. (New York: St Martin's Griffin, 2011).

on hoping? — the situation in which climate change is not only already underway, but actually has its own momentum that is now unstoppable. We can limit the damage if we act soon, but a lot of damage is inevitable, especially because climate change is bound to trigger other processes, like the release of the vast quantities of methane under the arctic tundra. We are already living in a different and tougher world, and it is bound to get tougher.

But McKibben insists that this is not an excuse to give up. Rather, we need the opposite: increased engagement. We must keep up the fight to prevent climate change getting even more out of control, but also "we need now to understand the world we've created, and consider — urgently — how to live in it. We can't simply keep stacking boulders against the change that's coming on every front: we need to figure out what parts of our lives and our ideologies we must abandon so that we can protect the core of our societies and civilizations."[3] (I would want to add: so that we can protect what we can of the rest of creation too.) This doesn't mean giving up hope, but it requires being mature and realistic about where we have got to and need to be going. "Maturity is not the opposite of hope; it's what makes hope possible."[4]

What, he argues, we must do has a lot in common with what the Transition movement is envisaging and working toward.[5] It means scaling down. It means getting more local than global. In comparison with modern so-called progress and its dreams of limitless growth of many kinds, it means decline. We will need, he says, "to focus not on growth but on maintenance, on a controlled decline from the perilous heights to which we've climbed."[6] If we are wise, we need not experience the sort of collapse that Jared Diamond's book documents for societies of the past. We can decline, McKibben says, "lightly, carefully, gracefully."[7] And it will bring some benefits of its own, such as the recovery of local community.

But then, what is the role of hope in such a scenario? I would suggest that hope's role will be to be *discerning* and *imaginative*. Discernment is

3. McKibben, *Eaarth*, p. xiv.

4. McKibben, *Eaarth*, p. xiv.

5. See, e.g., Rob Hopkins, *The Transition Companion: Making Your Community More Resilient in Uncertain Times* (Totnes: Green Books, 2011); Timothy Gorringe and Rosie Beckham, *Transition Movement for Churches* (Norwich: Canterbury Press, 2013).

6. McKibben, *Eaarth*, p. 204.

7. McKibben, *Eaarth*, p. 151.

partly about seeking out, spotting, and choosing the real possibilities for hope. Remember that hope is empowered by love, and remember also the old saying that love will find a way. The truth in the saying is that love may see what merely dispassionate surveys and calculations may miss. Love may be undeterred by the false realism that pours cold water on all our hopes. Love may find the real possibilities for hope — not unrealistic ones, but the ones that need some spotting and some work.

Another Old Testament story can make my point: David and Goliath (1 Samuel 17). Of all the unlikely things, the shepherd boy with his sling and his five stones from the brook brings down the giant no one else dares to confront. He refuses Saul's offer of weapons and armor, which would only weigh him down. He just uses his sling, and it proves to be precisely the way Goliath can be defeated. With a sling David is able to attack before he comes within range of Goliath's weapons, and with it he reaches the one exposed bit of Goliath's body: his forehead. So David's remarkable success is not a miracle in the ordinary sense. What is remarkable is that David did just the thing that was needed but that no one else thought of doing. David, confident that God was with him, did the only thing he knew how to do and the one thing likely to succeed. That's what discerning real possibilities for hope might be like.

Hope should be discerning, and it can also be *imaginative.* I don't mean fantasizing. Imagination has a much more serious role in human thinking than that. It opens up real possibilities. It suggests how we might do something quite differently. Giving up modern progressivism does not mean giving up human ingenuity and inventiveness. It does not mean giving up technology but adopting and developing appropriate technology. Not the big technological dreams for getting nature back under control. They are just moving on in the same direction that got us here in the fix we're in. We need technologies that suit our properly human place within a creation for which we should care, not enslave.

There are a lot of other things to think about. What are the priorities for conserving the nonhuman creatures when we cannot do everything? How can we scale down to a more localized life without abandoning global relationships and responsibilities in a world where the poorer countries are going to suffer most from what the rich nations have caused, and in a world where there are going to be climate refugees on a scale it is not easy to imagine the world coping with? And among all the manifold good things that we all busy ourselves with, what is really going to matter most? Must we focus more and prioritize?

In Conclusion

In a situation of disappointed and uncertain hope, it is the virtuous trio of faith, hope, and love that must keep us going. In the New Testament faith and hope are often linked with endurance.[8] We may need to be prepared for a lot of just keeping going, sticking it out, not giving up when it would be easy to. But faith, hope, and love, working, of course, with all the resources of knowledge and expertise that we can muster, must also lead us into new visions of the possible even within a sorely damaged world.

---

8. E.g., Rom. 5:3-4; Jas. 1:3; Rev. 13:10.

CHAPTER 9

Creation — Divine and Human:
An Old Testament Theological Perspective

(1) Creation — Divine and Human — according to George Steiner

George Steiner, in his remarkable book *Grammars of Creation*,[1] based on his 1990 Gifford lectures in Glasgow, takes the idea of the creation of the world by God as a kind of criterion with which to explore ideas of human creativity in the arts and sciences. Can artistic creation in reality be more than imitation? Unlike divine creation, which is *ex nihilo* ("out of nothing"), it is certainly arguable that no "art form . . . comes out of nothing. Always, it comes *after*. Modernism can be defined as an exasperation with this cruel fact of posteriority."[2] Yet, against all denials from viewpoints outside the aesthetic, Steiner insists on some quality of originality in great art, something we recognize as exceeding mere invention: "the simultaneously obvious and undefinable analogy with creation itself."[3] The creation of characters, he suggests, is "a close analogue to the divine creation of organic forms": they exhibit "the organic, the life-given autonomy of the begotten, rather than the assemblage, the combinatorial . . . which would characterize the invented. *Poiesis* . . . lays claim to primary making."[4] But in that case the artist rivals God, a theme Steiner had already stressed in his earlier book *Real Presences*.[5] He speaks of "the artist's sense of himself as 'counter-creator,' competing with the primal *fiat* . . . on ground at once

1. George Steiner, *Grammars of Creation* (London: Faber, 2001).
2. Steiner, *Grammars of Creation*, p. 19.
3. Steiner, *Grammars of Creation*, p. 93.
4. Steiner, *Grammars of Creation*, p. 144.
5. George Steiner, *Real Presences: Is There Anything in What We Say?* (London: Faber, 1989).

exultant and blasphemous,"[6] and recalls that Tolstoy felt just this sense of competing with God: "They were, as he put it, two bears wrestling in the forest."[7]

Elsewhere in the book Steiner also suggests that abstract art, especially when it incorporates emptiness, "takes us nearest to the fabric of creation,"[8] in that it evokes the infinity of possibilities out of which our particular universe is a selection. But Steiner does not think that art can actualize completely other possibilities out of this nothing. Art cannot create out of nothing; it is always "combinatorial," always combining preexisting elements, but it can do so in genuinely new and unprecedented ways, and such possible combinations are "almost unbounded."[9] I take him to mean that the possibilities of the given world (for believers, the world created by God out of nothing) are sufficiently vast, so many of them yet unrealized, as to enable what we recognize as artistic creation, distinguishable from invention. He offers this definition of such creation: "that which is enacted freedom and which includes and expresses in its incarnation the presence of what is absent from it or of what could be radically other."[10] In this definition creation has two essential attributes. One is freedom, the fact that a created thing "could not-have-been": "It is solely in this gratuity towards being — being is always a gift — that the artist, the poet, the composer can be thought 'god-like,' that their practice can be termed analogous to that of the First Maker."[11] This gratuitousness or contingency, that it "could not-have-been," distinguishes artistic creation from anything that occurs in the sciences. The second essential attribute of creation is that the work created communicates its contingency to us by means of imperfections: perfection would exclude the possibilities of not being or being otherwise.

Steiner appears to me to have argued that, while creation out of nothing is the exclusively divine act (in this sense: "Tautologically, only God creates"),[12] which cannot be rivaled by humans, still the given world is sufficiently open for the free choice of hitherto unrealized possibilities of that world to be possible. Such freedom and originality in artistic creations suggest to us the analogy with divine creation, and it is precisely this

6. Steiner, *Grammars of Creation,* p. 90.

7. Steiner, *Grammars of Creation,* p. 68.

8. Steiner, *Grammars of Creation,* p. 115.

9. Steiner, *Grammars of Creation,* p. 118.

10. Steiner, *Grammars of Creation,* p. 108.

11. Steiner, *Grammars of Creation,* p. 108.

12. Steiner, *Grammars of Creation,* p. 20.

analogy, with its evocation of the abyss of infinite possibilities behind the given world, that enables us to distinguish what we call creation from the merely mimetic qualities of invention.

This seems to be a thesis that invites exploration from a theological direction as well as others. In the limited scope of this essay, I shall explore the extent to which creation in the Old Testament is an exclusively and incomparably divine act, without human analogy, and the extent to which it may be open to human analogies. Michael Welker has criticized conventional theological concepts of creation as false abstractions from the much richer biblical descriptions.[13] Though my concerns now are different from his and will therefore focus on different features of the biblical material, I happily follow his example in attending to the detail of the texts and attempting to avoid premature abstraction from the texts. To this end it will be important also to look beyond Genesis to some of the many imaginative portrayals of creation elsewhere in the Old Testament.

(2) Creation as the Incomparable Divine Act

The first three words of the Bible are: *bere'shit bara' 'elohim,* "In the beginning God created . . ." Not many readers notice a remarkable feature of these words. In the Hebrew Bible the word "god" *('elohim)* does not always designate the one and only true God, though it usually does. However, the word "create" *(bara')* is a word that is used only with God as its subject — a remarkable fact to which theologians have given far too little attention. That the opening words of the Bible refer to the one and only true God is therefore made certain, not by the term used to refer to God himself, but by the word used to refer to his activity, a word that defines the uniquely divine relationship to the world. It is the one who created *(bara')* the heaven and the earth who is the one and only true God in the Bible's definition. If it is this Hebrew word that we render by "create," then Steiner's statement is quite strictly accurate: "Tautologically, only God creates."[14]

The verb *bara'* occurs forty-eight times in the Hebrew Bible, and in no case here or in later Hebrew (eleven occurrences in Ben Sira, thirty-eight in the Dead Sea Scrolls) does it have any subject other than God. This is extraordinary. I do not know another word in any language that

13. Michael Welker, *Creation and Reality* (Minneapolis: Fortress, 1999).
14. Steiner, *Grammars of Creation,* p. 20.

can be used only of God. Theologians are accustomed to think that all our language about God is analogical or metaphorical use of language that we also use of things in the world. Since God is not anything within the world, but the transcendent other, this language cannot have, when applied to God, the same meaning as it has when applied to things in the world. Its use is justified because we suppose there is an analogy in God to what the language says about things in the world, but at the same time there is difference. God is not good or wise in the same way that creatures are good or wise, and moreover we cannot specify the difference. Our ordinary language about God always embodies at the same time both what we can and what we cannot know of God. It is all qualified by divine transcendence.

A word that is only used of God would seem to be very problematic. How can we know what it means? By translating *bara'* as "create" or by translating it by any English word at all we avoid the problem. All possible translations of *bara'* are words that can also be used with creatures as the subject; we have no other English words to use. But if we only spoke Hebrew — or if we just took the word *bara'* into English without translating it — how could we know what this word that is only used of God means? Probably it once had a wider use and came to be used only of God, but we know nothing of that wider use. It would be a long-obsolete use that is unknown to the Hebrew Bible and not relevant to the meaning of *bara'* as it is used in the Hebrew language we know.

How can we know what *bara'* means? First, by observing that it is sometimes used in parallel with other verbs, especially the two other verbs that are most commonly used in the Hebrew Bible to refer to God's activity of creating: *'asah,* which is a very common word meaning "to make" or "to do" (2,622 times in the Hebrew Bible), and *yatsar,* which means "to form" (63 times in the Hebrew Bible, 42 of these with God as subject). These words are not simply synonyms, but the use of *bara'* in parallel with them implies that it shares some overlap of meaning with them. It must have the sense of bringing something into being or bringing something about.

Then, second, we can look at what it is that God is said to *bara'.* The verb is used not only of God's activity in the beginning, as in Genesis 1, but also of acts in history. In this latter usage we find that what God brings about *(bara')* are unprecedentedly new events (Num. 16:30; Isa. 41:20; 48:7; Jer. 31:22). For example, "I will do [*'asah*] marvels such as have not been brought about [*bara'*] in all the earth or in any nation" (Exod.

34:10). Whereas *'asah* could have been used of any act of God, *bara'* is used there only because what God promises to do is something completely unheard of. The reference is to novelty such as only God creates. It is something that cannot come simply from the ordinary possibilities of the creaturely, but only from the transcendent possibilities of God. The word *bara'* evidently points to what we can state only negatively about this kind of divine activity: that it does what cannot be done only with existing materials or conditions. I said "*only* with existing materials or conditions," because it is not always the case that *no* existing materials or conditions are involved at all. This was evidently not the case, for example, in God's creation of Israel, for which *bara'* is used (Isa. 43:1, 7, 15; Mal. 2:10). So we cannot say that the word *bara'* itself means "to create out of nothing" in the sense of the later notion of *creatio ex nihilo* (which is not stated as such in the Hebrew Bible or the New Testament). But it is surely significant that *bara'* is never used with an object or a prepositional phrase indicating material out of which God creates. In its use in the first Genesis creation narrative, it certainly comes rather close to the meaning "to create out of nothing."

If we now look more closely at that creation narrative (Gen. 1:1–2:4) we find that, in addition to the word *bara'*, there are also other ways of referring to God's activity in creating. In particular, there is the repeated formula: "God said, 'Let . . .' And it was so" (1:6-7, 9, 11, 14-15, 24, cf. 29-30). This uses the human analogy of speaking a word of command, but it transcends the human analogy in that the command itself effects what it commands. Instead of creatures obeying the command, creatures are brought into being by the command. The language is designed to disqualify precisely the human analogy it proposes. In one of these cases, there is no other account of how what is commanded comes about than the "And it was so" (1:9), but in three cases it is also said that God made *('asah)* (1:7, 16, 25), while in two cases there is no "And it was so" but instead God is said to have "created" *(bara')* (1:21, 27). These statements do not explain any further how the divine command effects what it commands; they simply repeat in other terms that God created the creatures in question.

More remarkable, perhaps, are two cases in which the creaturely agency of the earth is evidently involved in the fulfillment of the command:

And God said, "Let the earth put forth [literally: cause to shoot forth] vegetation. . . ." And it was so. The earth brought forth [literally: caused to go forth] vegetation. (1:11-12)

And God said, "Let the earth bring forth [literally: cause to go forth] living creatures of every kind. . . ." And it was so. God made ['*aśah*] the wild animals of every kind. (1:24-25)

Evidently some creaturely agency is not necessarily excluded from what is generally designated by the word *bara'*, but the creaturely agency is not regarded as sufficient.

The image of command has commonly been thought to indicate the freedom of God in creation and the contingency of the creation. According to Dietrich Bonhoeffer, "God *speaks:* this means that he creates in freedom and in his creating remains totally free vis-à-vis his work."[15] The vision of God the Creator in the book of Revelation interprets the Old Testament understanding of creation in the words of the twenty-four elders to God: "you created all things, and by your will they existed and were created" (4:11).

The first Genesis creation narrative seems to use the two verbs *bara'* and *'aśah* more or less interchangeably. They occur seven[16] and eight times respectively (*bara':* 1:1, 21, 27 [*tris*]; 2:3, 4; *'aśah:* 1:7, 16, 25, 26, 31; 2:2 [*bis*], 3), in the following pattern: ABBABBAAABBBABA.[17] It is notable that *bara'* not only frames the whole account in the introductory and concluding statements, but also, when used of individual acts of creation, begins and ends the acts of creation of living beings (1:21 and three times of the creation of humanity in 1:27). It seems clear that the very general word *'aśah* is subordinated to the word that stresses the incomparability of God's creating. *'Aśah* is so general that it does not add another image to that of God's word of command effecting what it commands, but it is notable that this creation account, unlike the second creation narrative in Genesis 2, avoids the word *yatsar*, which is elsewhere quite commonly used of creation by God. This is doubtless because *yatsar* conveys the image of forming with hands or fingers, a different image that would not sit easily alongside the image of speaking commands. It is often claimed that this creation account avoids *yatsar* as too anthropomorphic. Forming with hands is really no more anthropomorphic than speaking. But it is true, as we have observed, that the image of speaking a command is used in this

---

15. Dietrich Bonhoeffer, *Creation and Fall: A Theological Interpretation of Genesis 1–3,* trans. John C. Fletcher (London: SCM, 1959), p. 19.

16. I presume that 2:4a concludes the first creation narrative, rather than beginning the second, but this is disputed.

17. A = *bara'*, B = *'aśah*. See the table.

account in a way that transcends the human analogy. The same kind of disqualification of the analogy in the course of using it could probably not have been accomplished with *yatsar*.

Does this creation account teach creation out of nothing? This conceptuality as such, we must recognize, is foreign to the narrative. But the picture of chaos, if we can use that really-too-Hellenistic term for the *tohu vebohu* of Genesis 1:2, is not a description of preexisting matter out of which God created the world. This chaos has no potential to become anything. It is an emptiness of being that, when it reappears in the biblical story, can only be a power of destruction against all created being. It pictures the complete absence of preconditions for creation. In that sense this creation narrative affirms what the later formulation of creation out of nothing was designed to safeguard. As Robert Jenson puts it, " 'before' there is the creature there is God and nothing. Nor is this nothing of a kind that can be the antecedent condition of something. God's speaking is the creature's only antecedent condition."[18]

In summary, the first creation account seems designed to stress the incomparability of God's creative activity, and gives little encouragement to a notion of human creativity as in any way analogous to God's. It is not that the creatures in this account are merely passive objects of God's creative activity. The account stresses the extent to which God's creating and blessing empower the creatures' own activity: plants produce seed and trees fruit, sun and moon give light and rule and separate, living creatures multiply, humans have dominion and multiply. But reproduction is here described quite differently from creation: it is precisely not the unprecedented novelty that is attributed to God in the use of the word *bara'* that dominates this account.

However, this studied incomparability is not the only way the Hebrew Bible speaks of God's creative activity. It also speaks in ways that entail the comparability of God's creation with forms of human activity. We shall begin with an aspect of the first creation account itself that is evident only from its clear connection with another part of the Torah. We shall then turn to terminology and images of creation that occur in descriptions of and references to creation outside the first Genesis narrative.

18. Robert W. Jenson, *Systematic Theology,* Vol. II: *The Works of God* (New York: Oxford University Press, 1999), p. 12.

		First Genesis Creation Account: 1:1–2:4a			
Days 1-7	**Created**	**Creation formula**	*bara'*	*'aśah*	**other divine actions**
Introduction: 1:1-2			*bara'*		
Day 1: 1:3-5	Light	God said, Let . . .			divided
		And there was			named
Day 2: 1:6-8	Firmament	God said, Let . . .		*'aśah*	divided
		And it was so			named
Day 3: 1:9-13	Dry land	God said, Let . . .			
		And it was so			named
	Vegetation	God said, Let . . .			
		(earth bring forth)			
		And it was so			
		earth brought forth			
Day 4: 1:14-19	Heavenly bodies	God said, Let . . .			
		And it was so		*'aśah*	set
Day 5: 1:20-23	Sea creatures + birds	God said, Let . . .	*bara'*		blessed
Day 6: 1:24-31	Land creatures	God said, Let . . .			
		(earth bring forth)			
		And it was so		*'aśah*	
	Humans	God said, Let . . .		*'aśah*	
			bara'		
			bara'		
			bara'		blessed
					said, said
		And it was so		*'aśah*	
Day 7: 2:1-3	Sabbath rest			*'aśah*	finished
				'aśah	rested
					blessed
					hallowed
			bara'	*'aśah*	rested
Conclusion: 2:4a			*bara'*		

Pattern of use of *bara'* (A) and *'aśah* (B): ABBABBAAABBBABA

(3) Creation as Work

Although the first creation account in Genesis overwhelmingly stresses the incomparability of God's work of creation, there is also an implication that human work in some sense parallels this divine work. The pattern of six days of work followed by the Sabbath of rest suggests, without explicitly referring to, the same pattern of human work and rest later prescribed by God in the Sabbath commandment. According to Genesis 2:2-3,

> on the seventh day God finished the work [*mela'kah*] that he had done [*'aśah*], and he rested on the seventh day from all the work [*mela'kah*] that he had done. So God blessed the seventh day and hallowed it, because on it God rested from all the work [*mela'kah*] that he had done in creation.

The same word for "work" *(mela'akhah)* is used for human work in the Sabbath commandment (Exod. 20:9-10; 31:14-15), though in that context, despite the appeal to God's making and resting as the model for human behavior, this word itself is not used of God's work. More significant, however, is the fact that in the Sabbath commandment there is no occurrence of the verb *bara'*, the word that designates God's creative work as incomparable. The word used for human work *(mela'kah)* is the ordinary word for ordinary work, and so does not set up a parallel between God's work of creation and human creativity in any more specialized sense than the ordinary daily labor of most people. Thus the connection between the first Genesis creation amount and the Sabbath commandment in Exodus does indicate a parallel between God's work and human work, but it carefully avoids comparison of human work with the uniquely creative element in God's work of creation.

(4) Creation as Craftsmanship

Among the most common verbs used for creation, as well as *bara'* and *'aśah*, is *yatsar*, which means "to form," "to shape," "to fashion." It is used of all kinds of craftsmanship: metalwork, wood carving, and (most commonly) pottery. Therefore, unlike the apophatic *bara'* and the colorless *'aśah*, this word *yatsar*, when used of divine creation, conveys a concrete and anthropomorphic image, implying also material that God forms into a shape. The concreteness of the image is emphasized when reference is made to God's hands or God's fingers: "the dry land, which his hands have formed" (Ps. 95:5); "Your hands have made me and fashioned me" (Ps. 119:73). The same image can be evoked even without the verb *yatsar:* "the heavens, the work of your fingers" (Ps. 8:3; cf. Job 10:8-9). When *yatsar* is used of divine creation, its object may be "all things" (Jer. 10:16 = 51:19), the earth (Isa. 45:18; Jer. 33:2), the mountains (Amos 4:13; cf. Prov. 8:25), summer and winter (Ps. 74:17), Leviathan (Ps. 104:26), the human heart (Ps. 33:15), the human eye (Ps. 94:9), and the human spirit (Zech. 12:1).

In the second Genesis creation account, it is used of the creation both of the man (Gen. 2:7-8) and of the animals and birds (2:19). In both cases God is said to have formed the creature "out of the ground" *(min-ha'adamah),* which in the case of the man *(ha'adam)* is a pun. But the narrative of the man's creation specifies God's action even more explicitly: "he formed the man out of dust from the ground" (2:7). Here the second creation narrative differs sharply from the first account's scrupulous avoidance of the idea that God created out of anything. We should probably not think here of the potter's production of vessels, a routine creation of relatively standard objects, but rather of the production of clay figures of human beings, such as are known from the ancient Near East. This is the crafting of a work of art: God is portrayed as a sculptor. It has been suggested that when God subsequently creates the woman from the man's rib — "God built [*banah*] the rib into a woman" (2:22) — the analogy is with the technique of making clay figurines out of reeds and clay, the reeds forming "bones" to support the clay that is molded around them. The narrative steps beyond the analogy of human craftsmanship when God brings the clay figure to life by breathing into it (2:7). Humans and other creatures revert to dust when God withdraws this breath (Ps. 104:29; cf. Gen. 3:19; Job 10:9; Ps. 90:3).

(5) Creation as Building

Another quite frequent image of creation depicts God as the architect-builder of the universe. (In ancient Israel the master builder both designed and built.) One of the most vivid descriptions is in the great divine speech to Job:

> Where were you when I laid the foundation of the earth?
> Tell me, if you have understanding.

> Who determined its measurements — surely you know!
> Or who stretched a measuring line across it?
> On what were its bases sunk,
> or who laid its cornerstone
> when the morning stars sang together
> and all the heavenly beings shouted for joy? (Job 38:4-7)

Elsewhere God is described as laying the foundations of the earth (Ps. 102:25; cf. Prov. 8:29), fixing the beams on which the upper story rests (Ps. 104:3; cf. Amos 9:6), using calipers to mark out the boundary between light and darkness (Job 26:10; cf. Prov. 8:27). God built with his own hands (Isa. 48:13), since it was he alone who erected the universe — with perhaps only the help of his wisdom (Prov. 8:30, if the correct translation is "I was beside him, like a master worker").

This image of creation as building has a special interest for our concern with Steiner's claim that human creativity in its strongest sense is an attempt to rival God, a kind of countercreation. Steiner rarely mentions architecture, but in the Bible two signal and connected instances in which a human creative enterprise expresses human hubris, an attempt at self-achievement that rivals God, concern building. The first is the Tower of Babel (Genesis 11), a building soaring up to heaven, an attempt to rival the divine architecture of the universe. The second concerns the later city of Babylon, Babel's namesake and historical successor. In Daniel 4, Nebuchadnezzar, king of Babylon, boasts of his creation: "Is this not magnificent Babylon, which I have built as a royal capital by my mighty power and for my glorious majesty?" (4:30). It is for this blasphemous hubris that he is struck down with madness and lives like the wild animals until he learns to acknowledge his dependence on the sovereignty of God.

(6) Creation as Making Camp

Because of the Bible's commonsense world picture, according to which the sky is a great dome over the circular flat earth, God's creation of the heavens could be depicted as pitching a tent:

> He stretches out the heavens like a canopy,
> and spreads them like a tent to live in. (Isa. 40:22)

This is the meaning of the quite frequent expression: God "stretched out the heavens" (Ps. 104:2; Isa. 44:24; 45:12). Once again, references to God's hands make the image especially concrete and vivid (Isa. 45:12). A fuller picture probably depicts the earth as the carpet spread out on the floor of the tent:

> I am the LORD, who made all things,
> who alone stretched out the heavens,
> who by myself spread out the earth. (Isa. 44:24)

(7) Creation as Begetting and Giving Birth

The Bible largely avoids images that would portray the world as derived biologically from God as its parent, but there seems to be at least one passage that imagines God as a mother giving birth to the world:

> Before the mountains were born,
> or you [God] were in travail with the earth and the world,
> from everlasting to everlasting you are God. (Ps. 90:2)

Another text that should be mentioned here is Genesis 4:1, which describes the first human birth. When Eve gives birth to Cain, she says, "I have acquired [*qanah*] a man by means of YHWH." The verb *qanah* is here a punning explanation of the name Cain *(qayin)*. The verb usually means "to acquire," but there are a few instances in which it means "to create" or perhaps "to beget" (Deut. 32:6; Prov. 8:22). In particular, in Genesis 14 it is used to describe Melchizedek's God as "God Most High, maker of heaven and earth" (14:19, 22). So the sense of Eve's cry of pride and joy may be that she too has created a man, as hitherto only God had done. Of course, her creation of a man is not independent of God, but only by God's enabling. Eve, whom Genesis has called "the mother of all the living" (3:20), celebrates her participation in the life-giving work of God. Procreation is seen as participation in creation, though not as in any way contradicting the Old Testament's many affirmations that each conception is a creative act of God himself (e.g., Ps. 139:13-16; Job 10:8-12). This text seems to me the closest the Bible gets to modern talk of humans as "cocreators" with God, but hardly enough to warrant such language.

(8) Conclusions

We have not exhausted the diverse wealth of biblical imagery for creation, but we have seen that there is much that is excluded by the first Genesis creation account, with its massive insistence on the uniqueness and incomparability of the divine creative activity. This account has priority, not only in canonical sequence but surely also in theological significance. Only when we have recognized that there is a transcendent uniqueness to the act of creation, without which God would not be God nor creatures creatures, can we then explore the subordinate senses in which there may be human, creaturely activities that bear some analogy to and remind us of the divine creation. Of the images we have considered, craftsmanship and building bring us closest to Steiner's concerns. Of course, these work in the reverse direction: from the human activity to God's pictured as analogous, not from God's creation to human activities that resemble it. But the use of the images certainly does entail that these human activities in some way resemble the divine activity of creation.

However, we have by no means fully legitimated Steiner's argument from scriptural precedent. I do not see evidence that the Bible actually envisages human activity that goes beyond the mimetic to the kind of originality that Steiner is attempting to identify in great art. Recall that Steiner is speaking of an originality in human creation that, while it is not actually creation out of nothing, is distinguishable from invention because it does suggest to us the divine creation out of nothing. I do not find anything of that sort in the Old Testament. So this essay leaves Steiner's argument still in quest of theological validity.

CHAPTER 10

God's Embrace of Suffering

Introduction — Envisaging Undeserved Suffering

On March 11, 2011, a massive earthquake and tsunami devastated northwest Japan, killing about 28,000 people and making hundreds of thousands of people homeless. As a physical phenomenon the earthquake was the most severe in modern Japanese history, though it was not actually the most catastrophic. (More than 100,000 people died in the Tokyo earthquake of 1923.) Of natural disasters on this scale, it has been the most fully recorded — both by scientific monitoring and by photography and film, including the extraordinary footage filmed on mobile phones as the great wave of the tsunami approached at great speed. But the pictures that perhaps especially brought home the scale of the disaster were those of the aftermath: miles and miles of brown mud where flourishing towns had stood, the wreckage of buildings and possessions scattered here and there but dwarfed by the expanses of newly created wasteland. In the past few years I have visited both Hiroshima and Nagasaki, and these pictures of the ruin the tsunami left in its wake reminded me of nothing more than the pictures of the wasteland that was Hiroshima and Nagasaki after a very different kind of disaster. Many people have commented how peculiarly sad it would be if Japan, the only country that has so far suffered both the annihilating power and the long-term effects of atomic bombs, were also to suffer on a large scale the effects of radiation from the Fukushima Daiichi nuclear power plant. The effects have been limited, but it is still not clear how serious the long-term prospects may be.

It is striking that it was the same kind of natural disaster — a massive earthquake followed by a huge tsunami — that stands symbolically at the beginning of the modern discussion of theodicy in Europe: the 1755 Lisbon earthquake, which may have been of similar magnitude to the March 11 earthquake in Japan, and caused the death of up to 50,000 people in Portugal, Spain, and North Africa. This tsunami made an impact as far away as the west coast of Ireland. The catastrophe served, among many Enlightenment thinkers, notably Voltaire, to refute the optimistic theodicy of Leibnitz, who famously said that all is for the best in the best of all possible worlds. All was certainly not for the best.

It was as a natural disaster for which humans could not be held responsible that the Lisbon earthquake made its point against blandly optimistic theodicies. In the twentieth century, discussion of the so-called problem of suffering was influenced more by the appalling scale of human evil seen in the Holocaust, in Stalin's massacres, in the bombing of Hiroshima and Nagasaki, in Cambodia and Ruanda, and other horrors of modern history. In the twenty-first century, beginning with the Boxing Day tsunami of 2004, natural catastrophe has so far loomed larger than human evil. The problem of suffering as an argument against belief in God was raised in the western media after the Boxing Day tsunami, though not, it seems, by the victims of the catastrophe, many of whom were sustained and enabled to hope by their religious faith. But an important aspect of the impact made by earthquakes and tsunamis is the point they make, not so much against theodicy as against the more humanistic modern Western faith in technology. Like climate change, they are a brutal reminder that we have not in fact mastered the forces of nature and bent them to our wills and desires — nor are we likely to do so.

It is true that natural disasters are often exacerbated or even caused by human activity, as in the case of the effects of climate change. The Boxing Day tsunami would not have affected coastal areas such as those of Thailand so badly had the vegetation that formed a natural protection not been cleared away to make room for tourism. But in the case of the March 11 earthquake and tsunami, as far as I can see, if we leave the nuclear factor out of account, there was nothing that could have been done to ameliorate the impact (unless, of course, Japanese people stopped living in areas likely to be affected by earthquakes and tsunamis, but this is hardly a practical suggestion). The Japanese build in such a way as to minimize danger from earthquakes; they have good early warning systems; people expect earthquakes and are well prepared. But in the face of such massive forces of nature, Japanese organization and technical expertise were even more helpless than the fishing boats in Katsushika Hokusai's famous painting

The Wave off Kanagawa. (Though the wave is probably not a tsunami, this painting certainly expresses awe at the power of the ocean.)

The governor of Tokyo, Shintaro Ishihara, called the tsunami divine judgment visited upon Japan as punishment for "the egoism, which has attached itself like rust to the mentality of the Japanese people over a long period of time," though in the face of public outrage he quickly retracted this statement and apologized. It is true that the Old Testament prophets not uncommonly saw natural disaster as God's judgment on human sin, but perhaps one has to be a prophet to do so. Certainly no one has the right to suppose that Japan deserves a tsunami any more than their own country does. There is a category of undeserved suffering, a category that is not to be rejected on the grounds that no one is innocent of sin (except very small children, many of us would want to add). Perhaps we all deserve tsunamis, but they do not seem to be allocated fairly, any more than the effects of global warming will be (indeed, have already been).

Does undeserved suffering belong within the scope of atonement theology? I take that question to mean: does it belong within God's great project of putting the world to rights through the life, death, resurrection, and future coming of Jesus?

The Scope of Atonement

The Christian doctrine of atonement presupposes that there is something deeply — not just superficially, but deeply — wrong with the human condition. The diagnosis has broadly three aspects. (1) There is moral evil, which means not simply the evil we do and bear responsibility for, but the fact that there is something deeply wrong with *us*, individually and socially, something that needs more than good advice and education to cure. (2) There is meaningless suffering, tragedy, and what the book of Ecclesiastes calls vanity or emptiness. This does not seem just to be something wrong with us as moral agents (though much undeserved suffering is caused by human acts), but something deeply wrong with how things are in this world. (3) There is death, which is not just a biological necessity, though it is that, but something deeply unsatisfactory that threatens the value of human persons. But, at the deepest root of these three elements in a Christian diagnosis of what we need liberating from, there is a common factor. The deepest dimension of all three facets of what is wrong is the lack of God. In the evil we cannot help contributing to, in the meaningless tragedy of life, and in the inconsolableness of death, what we miss is the love at the heart of reality. When we do evil we turn our back on that love; when we experience evil that love seems to turn its back on us. Either we have forsaken God or God has forsaken us. Death may come to us either as God's verdict on our failure or as God's abandonment of us, leaving us to perish. When we go to the depths of what is wrong with human life, in every case what we find is alienation from God, who is the love at the heart of all reality and the life that sustains all reality. This alienation from God is what much of our culture most of the time succeeds in hiding from us, while the "new atheism" makes a virtue of it.

If the diagnosis is right, then what we need more than anything and in every part of our lives is to find God. In a Christian doctrine of atonement this is only possible if God finds us — that is, if God finds us where we are in the depths of our alienation from God. That happens on the cross, where in Jesus' dying cry of agony and godforsakenness he himself plumbs the depths of the human plight — so that the love of God can reach those who are in those depths. We shall return to this shortly.

In the Western tradition of atonement theology the focus has been on guilt and our need of forgiveness and on evil as a power of compulsion to sin from which we need liberation. In the Greek fathers and the Eastern tradition the focus has been more on mortality and our need of eternal life, which is participation in the eternal livingness of God. The meaningless tragedy in which God seems to leave people to suffer for no apparent reason has not figured very much in the theological tradition before the modern period. The sense that in the cross those who suffer, whether or not by their own fault, find God with them in suffering, healing their abandonment, has probably been much more a feature of Christian spirituality than of formal theology.

Does it, however, have any basis in the New Testament? Is not the cross in the New Testament overwhelmingly understood in relation to sin and death, not undeserved suffering — except in the sense that Jesus, who did not deserve suffering on his own account, submitted to it for the sake of those who did and do?

The Passion of Jesus and the Psalms of Lament

One feature of the passion narratives in the Gospels is worthy of our attention in this connection. All four of them make many and unmistakable allusions to (and even quotations from) the psalms of lament, those psalms in which the psalmist cries out to God from the midst of suffering, not only seeking deliverance but frequently also questioning why he/she is suffering, why God has abandoned the psalmist, leaving him/her to suffer. In these psalms of lament there are only rare references to sin that could be understood as the cause of God's inaction. Most protest against apparently undeserved suffering. They are not only psalms of lament but also psalms of complaint and protest.

In Mark's narrative (followed by Matthew) the connection with such psalms is the more visible and significant because here Jesus' dying words, cited in Jesus' native Aramaic, are the opening words of Psalm 22: "My God, my God, why have you forsaken me?" These words express both the intimacy of Jesus' relation to his Father (in the double "My God") and the reality of his abandonment (which is not just a feeling). I do not think that these allusions to the psalms are a case simply of fulfillment of messianic prophecy (though that is especially important in John), as though the psalms are being read as prophecies of what the Messiah as an individual is to suffer. For one thing, Jewish Christians would have been well used to the praying of these psalms as giving voice to the experience of whoever found them relevant to their case. But nor is Jesus just one righteous person who, just like others, voices his anguish in the words of the psalms. Mark certainly means more than that, as the many allusions to the psalms of lament in his passion narrative show. In Mark's narrative the psalms are being understood in a messianic way, but in the sense of an inclusive, not exclusive messianism. By that I mean that Jesus in his passion is identified with all who had prayed or could pray these psalms for themselves, all who suffer the meaningless abandonment from which they cry to God. Jesus identifies with them as his messianic destiny to suffer as they did on their behalf. He does not need, on his own account, an answer to the question "Why?" but he makes the question his own, speaking not in the Hebrew of the psalm but in his own Aramaic, in an act of loving solidarity with all who question why God has left them to suffer.[1]

---

1. I have argued this case more fully in *Jesus and the God of Israel: God Crucified and Other Studies on the New Testament's Christology of Divine Identity* (Grand Rapids: Eerdmans, 2008), chap. 8 ("God's Self-Identification with the Godforsaken in the Gospel of Mark").

The Cross and the Story of Jesus

To understand more adequately this loving solidarity of Jesus with all who suffer we need to avoid isolating the cross, as theories of atonement have too often done, from the total story of Jesus — both before and after his death. In the first place, Jesus' death can only be understood as God's loving solidarity with all who suffer if we read it in the light of the incarnation (and all the Gospels, in my view, recognize the divine identity of Jesus). The incarnation is God's radical self-identification with humanity, the act in which God enters human history as himself a human and identifies not merely with humanity in the ideal or the abstract, but with humanity as it concretely is, in its sinful and suffering condition. Jesus begins to make that loving identification with humanity in an intentional and public way when he submits to baptism by John the Baptist. He comes for baptism, not because he needs to repent and receive forgiveness on his own account, but as an act of messianic solidarity with his people Israel. This is the outset of a ministry of bringing God's love into people's lives by a practice of loving identification. Jesus understands people's selves and situations empathetically, with the sort of love that is not mere benevolence from a distance but that engages with people where they are and thereby makes a transformative difference. In the Gospel narratives his loving identification is with all sorts of people: women and men, children, poor people, wealthy people, sick people, disabled people, outcasts, the dregs of society, the people who ran society, the religious and the irreligious, the people who thought they were righteous, the people who knew they were sinners. He treated all these people differently because they were indeed all different. But especially he identified in understanding compassion with the people who knew the depths in one way or another: the mad, the despairing, the chronically sick, the utterly destitute, the outcasts, the notorious sinners — all the people who knew too well their forsakenness by God or who were often enough reminded by others that they had turned their backs on God. To the people who knew the depths Jesus enacted God's loving identification with them, bringing forgiveness, healing, new hope, and life out of death.

The cry of godforsakenness from the cross is the final, climactic point of Jesus' loving identification with all. He enters the human situation at its negative extreme. He does so not as just one more human being, ending up by force of circumstance where so many others do, but by choice, in obedience to his Father's will, in order to bring God's love for all the forsaken precisely into that extremity of abandonment by God. If God is to be found there, then there is no dimension of the human plight in which he cannot be found.

It may be important to stress that the cross, understood in this way in the context of the biblical story, is not merely an example or illustration of God's loving identification with all people in every aspect of the human plight. Jesus *enacts* God's love. His cross is God's definitive act of solidarity with all who suffer. It is as the crucified one, who really entered their darkness then and there and still bears the marks of it, that Jesus is, as the Japanese Catholic novelist Shusaku Endo puts it, "the eternal companion" of those who suffer.[2]

Does It Help?

If Jesus' loving identification with those who suffer, as I have expounded it, is presented as a response (though certainly not a solution) to the problem of undeserved suffering, one could ask the question: How does that help? What good is it to those who suffer to realize that Jesus is in the same boat with them? It certainly doesn't abolish the suffering. But it can, as Jürgen Moltmann puts it, remove "the suffering in suffering."[3] The "suffering in suffering" is the abandonment, the sense of being left to suffer, the lack of love. It is not difficult to appreciate, on a human level, that someone close to a person who suffers, someone who loves them with understanding empathy, who enters to some degree into the situation of the one who suffers because they choose to do so out of love, can help the person who suffers bear their suffering, can take some of the load from them. But deep in the heart of suffering is the sense of being abandoned by love itself, by the love at the heart of reality, by God. Even those who have experienced abandonment by all human companions can find strength and encouragement in the companionship of the crucified Christ.

It seems peculiarly appropriate to cite Shusaku Endo at the present time. In some of his novels and in his *Life of Jesus,* Endo tried to develop an appropriately Japanese form of Christian faith, some aspects of which

2. Shusako Endo, *A Life of Jesus,* trans. Richard A. Schuchert (New York: Paulist, 1978), pp. 85-86.

3. Jürgen Moltmann, *The Crucified God,* trans. R. A. Wilson and John Bowden (London: SCM, 1974), p. 46.

in its Western versions he found uncomfortable, like an ill-fitting suit of clothes, in a Japanese context.[4] One of his characters, Otsu, who learned his Christian theology in Europe but found it alien to his Japanese way of thinking, explains why he nevertheless remains a follower of Jesus: "I haven't been able to adapt myself to the thinking and the theology of Europe, but when I suffer all alone, I can feel the smiling presence of [Jesus], who knows all my trials."[5]

Endo is very conscious that the love of Jesus as he represents it, as a suffering with people that cannot make a material difference to the conditions that cause their suffering, appears weak and ineffectual in worldly terms, and sees this as the reason for the eventual rejection of Jesus by those who had enthusiastically hailed him as Messiah. Endo's is a rather bleak theology that offers no reason to hope for the alleviation of suffering by removing its causes. Both liberation theologians and charismatic Christians, for different reasons, would especially find him too close to a passive acquiescence in suffering, to the sort of fatalism that saps any attempt to improve things. Perhaps this is related to what the Western commentators, reporting the aftermath of the tsunami, have been calling Japanese stoicism. But if you live in a country in which earthquakes are frequent, you may be more aware than many of us Westerners are of the unavoidability of some kinds of suffering and the need simply to cope with them.

There is a difficult path to be trodden (difficult at least in theory) between protest against suffering and some kind of acceptance of such suffering as just having to be borne. It is a luxury of the modern West, perhaps, to be able to put all the emphasis on protest and activism. But, if one thinks, for example, of the suffering of those who suffer oppression in an unjust system, one can see how a sense of the solidarity of Jesus Christ with them in their sufferings can enable them to resist the dehumanizing effects of their suffering, to resist the deprivation of identity and dignity that their oppressors impose, to escape despair and to embrace hope. This is impressively evidenced in the spirituals of American black slaves.

However, it was not in the cross of Christ alone that those black slaves found solace and strength, but also in his resurrection and his future coming, which gave them hope for liberation from slavery. This is the other side of understanding the cross within the story of Jesus, which did not end

---

4. Emi Mase-Hasegawa, *Christ in Japanese Culture: Theological Themes in Shusaku Endo's Literary Works,* Brill's Japanese Studies Library 28 (Leiden: Brill, 2008), p. 78.

5. Shusako Endo, *Deep River,* trans. Van C. Gessel (London: Hodder, 1995), p. 119.

with his death. Just as Jesus died in loving solidarity with all who suffer, so he rose from death still in solidarity with them, as God's promise of a new future for them. Hope may be difficult in suffering, but it is also most alive in suffering, and the resurrection of Jesus enables that lively and active hope in those who know his loving solidarity with them.

The Im/passibility of God

To speak of the cross as God's suffering solidarity with all who suffer raises the dogmatic question: Is not God, by nature, immune from suffering? So we cannot leave the subject without some consideration of the orthodox tradition of Christology and its implications for the doctrine of God.

In the incarnation of God in Jesus Christ, the eternal Son, the second person of the Trinity, becomes the subject of all the activity and experience of Jesus. The fully human reality of Jesus' human experience is essential to real incarnation. That is Chalcedonian Christology. We should be quite clear that it requires both that we attribute every aspect of the human suffering of Jesus to the eternal Son and also that we recognize that such suffering, precisely human suffering in all its very human reality, entailing the frailty and vulnerability of human physicality, human emotions, and thinking, can be experienced by God only in incarnation. God in his eternal being cannot be thirsty or fear death or suffer the mockery of tormentors, but in Jesus he really does suffer precisely those things.

Yet if incarnation, with all that it entails by way of human suffering and other human experience, is possible for God, then it cannot be that God is absolutely impassible (unable to suffer) in the way that some, at least, of the theological tradition seems to imply. The Fathers really struggled to maintain both the reality of the incarnation and the impassibility of God that seemed to them necessary for God to be God. God the Son "suffered impassibly," said Cyril of Alexandria, and meant perhaps something like this: The eternal Son acknowledges the sufferings of his human nature as his own, but does not experience them as suffering. The flaw in this is that unless *someone* suffers there is no suffering. At most one might speak of damage. And Cyril, unlike the Antiochene theologians, was quite clear that there is only one acting subject in Christ — the divine Son.

If we insist, as I think orthodox Christology must, that God really suffers in incarnation, might we go on to attribute some kind of suffering to God outside incarnation? One reason for doing so arises when we put the cross in a trinitarian context, as we certainly need to do but as I have not so far done. In Romans 8:32 Paul looks, as it were, upon the crucified Jesus dying in abandonment by God, not from our perspective, but from God the Father's perspective. God, he says, "did not spare his own Son, but gave him up for us all." There is real pain in those words. As Moltmann puts it, not only does God the Son suffer abandonment by his Father, but the Father also suffers the death of his Son when he leaves him to die.[6] The two forms of suffering are different, but what could "did not spare his own Son" mean at all if it involved no pain? The analogy with what a human father would feel for his beloved son loses any meaning if we are to think of the Father acting dispassionately, unaffected by his loss of the Son. We would also be rather close to that degenerate kind of atonement doctrine that divides the Son who loves us from the Father who does not.

Is God then passible, as many theologians of the twentieth and twenty-first centuries would say, dissenting from the theological tradition? By way of responding briefly to this question, I will make three important points.

First, the doctrine of divine impassibility is a denial not merely that God can suffer but that God can be in any way affected by his creation. The relation between God and the world is understood as a purely one-way relationship in which God affects the world but is in no way affected by it. God's love, on this view, is not a relational involvement with others but a purely active benevolence. He can be neither adversely nor positively affected by the world. Even the incarnation must be conceived as an activity of God in the world that makes no difference to God. This is a view of God that most Christians throughout most of Christian history would, it seems to me, simply not recognize as the God they know in Christian prayer and practice, let alone as the God of the Bible.

Second, if we affirm divine passibility we must be very careful in specifying the sort of suffering that is possible for God. It is the voluntary suffering of love. God is not subject to suffering against his will, as we are. God does not suffer out of weakness, as we do. He suffers out of the fullness of his love for us. He suffers the suffering entailed by the relationship of love into which he has voluntarily opted by creating and relating to his creation. The Fathers, when they discussed impassibility, usually worked with a simple contrast between humans, who suffer unwillingly out of weakness, and God, who is not subject to anything. They failed to

---

6. Moltmann, *The Crucified God*, pp. 242-43, and frequently in his later writings.

recognize this particular sort of suffering — the voluntary suffering of love — that both humans and God can undertake purely for love.

Third, all our talk of God is analogical. We can only speak of God by analogy with created, especially human, things. To say that God loves is to say that there is something sufficiently like human love in the divine reality to make the word meaningful, but there is always also a difference. God does not love just like us, but we cannot specify the difference. To say that God undertakes the voluntary suffering of love is to say that God does something sufficiently like what humans do when we say that of them for the language to be meaningful. It truly tells us something about God, but there also has to be an unspecifiable difference, or God would not be God. It does not help to say that the difference is that in our case we suffer but in God's case he does not. That amounts to discarding analogy and claiming we know the difference. The appropriate path is to say that God suffers, while remembering that this, like all our talk of God, is analogical.

CHAPTER 11

The Christian Way as Losing and Finding Self

I chose this topic as one that could contribute to mutual understanding between Christians and Buddhists. Buddhism seems to me a religion focused exclusively on the transformation of self (recall the Buddha's refusal to answer questions not directly related to this), whereas Christianity appears to me rather as a religion that is about all kinds of things, perhaps because it is primarily about God. But, whether or not this contrast is valid, it is certainly true that Christianity is also vitally concerned with the transformation of the self.

This is not an easy topic to discuss. The definition and nature of the human self have been the subject of considerable discussion by philosophers and psychologists as well as theologians, and the results have been very varied. To achieve clarity in discussion of concepts of the self seems extremely difficult, and I do not expect to do so in this short essay. I will offer a preliminary account of the self that seems to me appropriate to Christian teaching and experience, though I do not claim that this is what Christian thinkers have always explicitly said about the self. The self is a unique and particular center of personal identity that can be characterized as relational and narratival. It is relational in that it is formed in personal and also nonpersonal relationships. (By the latter I mean relationships with sentient beings that are not persons and with nonsentient creatures too.) That is, it is formed in relationship with God, with other people, both intimately and socially, and with the rest of creation. It is narratival in that it is formed in and through time and finds its unique identity in a story with

---

Note: This essay originated as a contribution to a day of Buddhist-Christian dialogue.

past, present, and expected future. The human self has no independent being, outside of relationships, and no timeless existence outside of the temporal reality that we can only describe in narrative. I am who I am in my relationships with others, and I am who I become in the narrative of my life. From the Christian perspective, I believe, these make me who I really and truly am, the self that, redeemed and healed in every way, God will finally take into eternity.

The self exists within, indeed is part of, the flux of events in this temporal, spatial, and material reality. It is therefore characterized by both continuity and difference. There are major discontinuities in the life of the human self that might put in question the claim to continuous identity. I suggest that from the Christian perspective there are two kinds of discontinuity, and that an account of these may best highlight comparisons and contrasts between Christian and Buddhist teaching about the self.

First, there is the transformation of self that occurs in the transition from the false self to the true self. This is the transition that occurs decisively in Christian conversion, symbolized in baptism as a ritual act of dying and rising to new life, but which also must continue to occur throughout Christian life in this world, as continual experience of repentance and renewal. There are a variety of ways in which biblical and Christian language speaks of this transition. Paul speaks of dying to sin, and also of having been crucified with Christ and rising to new life in Christ. We shall return to this connection with Jesus Christ. But at this point it is most important to identify the difference between the old, sinful self that is left behind and the new, authentic self that one becomes.

Since selfhood is relational and narratival, the false self exists in severely distorted forms of relationship and narrative. This is the selfish and self-centered self that sees life only from the point of view of its own self-interest. Crucially, it places itself in the center, where God belongs, displacing God, and treating other people and the rest of creation as merely means to the self's own ends. Its relationships therefore are not loving but merely instrumental. It is *incurvatus in se,* turned in on itself, focused on its own self-concern, closed to the true reality of God, of others, and of creation. Instead of living in truly interdependent relationships, the false self would like to create itself, make itself the subject of a freely created narrative directed to its own ends. Thus, for the conversion of the false self, it is necessary for its story to be radically ruptured by the grace of God. The authentic self cannot evolve out of the false self but must be given by God.

By contrast, the true self is the selfless self, existing in self-giving to

God and to others, living for God and for others, realizing itself to be given by God and by others. It is not self-created but God-given. Its world is radically reordered, with God, the source and the goal of all things, at the center. This means that the true self lives, in a sense, from and to a center outside itself. As a unique and particular individual, it has its particular place in reality, from which it must view and relate to the rest of reality. Its perspective is relative to its own spatial, temporal, and material location in the world, as must be true of all finite creatures. But it can transcend this perspective through its openness to God and to others — its loving obedience to God, its empathic, loving identification with other people, its loving appreciation of all creatures. Its identity is formed in these relationships of love, so that its own concerns are taken up into the divine concern for all creation.

As for the narratival aspect of this self, the common images of rising from death to new life or of being reborn to a new kind of life convey the sense of a radically new beginning, a story that now arises from God's grace. This is what Paul means in the statement, often quoted in Buddhist-Christian dialogue, "I have been crucified with Christ; and it is no longer I who live, but it is Christ who lives in me" (Gal. 2:19-20). This does not mean that there is no longer a unique personal subject, no self at all, but that instead of Paul's pre-Christian attempt at self-creation, living from his own resources, he now lives from the grace of God in Christ. This is clear from the way he continues: "the life I now live in the flesh I live by faith in the Son of God, who loved me and gave himself for me" (Gal. 2:20). We shall return to the christological aspect of this.

But is this new identity wholly discontinuous with the old? Paul here comes as close to suggesting that as he can, but even here there is a continuity of Paul's "I" without which his claim would not make sense. There is continuity, but it is not a continuity the self maintains for itself through its transformation. It is continuity given by God in the grace that transforms the self. The false self and its world were never, of course, entirely false from start to finish; they were a sinful distortion of God's good creation. God's grace does not simply replace, it reforms and renews, it takes what is good of the old, what is redeemable of the old, into the new. Even those Christians who undergo the most revolutionary kind of conversion experience subsequently find that their awareness of a completely fresh start is consistent with realizing how much of what they previously were has gone into the making of the new. The old self's self-serving narrative has to be written, seen, and evaluated from a new perspective, but it cannot be disowned. It becomes itself part of a new narrative of grace. Paul's identity will forever be that of the persecutor of God's people who became, through God's disruption of that narrative, quite the opposite.

There is also another kind of discontinuity in the Christian understanding and experience of the self. This is not transition from false to true, but a feature of the true self's narrative. It is memorably expressed in a saying of Jesus that occurs no less than six times in the four Gospels.[1] In most occurrences there are interpretative additions to the saying, but in its simplest form it is:

> Whoever seeks to gain their life will lose it,
> but whoever loses their life will keep it. (Luke 17:33)

The Greek word here used for "life" *(psyche)* strongly approaches the meaning "self," so long as the self is understood to exist in the concrete life of the individual in relationships and history.

The first line describes the mistake made by the person who embraces their false self. The attempt to secure one's life by living it for one's own benefit is bound to fail, because death comes to everyone and is the end of what the selfish person is trying to keep. To live one's life as though one owns it and can use it and keep it for oneself is an illusion that death will brutally destroy, as the rich fool in Jesus' parable discovered. That life is given by God and cannot be secured but only received from him emerges undeniably but too late when God takes it back at death (Luke 12:16-21). But there is also a sense in which living for oneself destroys life already before death. In grasping and hoarding life for their own enjoyment, selfish people find the real fulfillment they seek escapes them even before life itself escapes them in death. The true self cannot be found that way.

The second line describes, by contrast, the way of the true self. Those who give up the foolish attempt to keep their lives for themselves, who, in other words, deny themselves and live for God and for others, find their lives given back to them by God. Does this finding of life (as in some versions of the saying) or keeping of life (in other versions) occur before or after death? The various contexts in which the Gospels place the saying show that they certainly envisage martyrdom, as the extreme case of losing one's life, but some of the contexts require a broader application to the

---

1. There are probably four independent traditions of the saying: (1) Mark 8:35; Matt. 16:25; Luke 9:24; (2) Matt. 10:39; (3) Luke 17:33; (4) John 12:25.

renunciation of self throughout a life of discipleship to Jesus (see especially Luke 9:23-24).

Intriguingly, with whichever sense of losing life one starts, one finds it includes the other also. Take, first, the person who expends their life in self-giving for God and for others. This is the life that is possible through radical trust in God, not needing to secure oneself through selfish clinging to life because one has entrusted oneself wholly to God. Such a person finds their true self in such self-giving. They find their true self continuously given them by God as they give themselves for God. But for someone who so lives out of trust in God, it is inconceivable that the extreme act of self-giving, the death of a martyr, should fall outside the scope of the saying. If self-giving is the way to true life, then a fortiori, should it be required of one, martyrdom must be.

Alternatively, one can begin with the saying's reference to martyrdom. Someone who gives up their life in the service of Christ entrusts their life to the power and faithfulness of God. All self-concern is transcended through faith in God. The one who thus gives their life will find it given back by God in resurrection beyond death. But if the receiving of one's true and eternal self is thus through the giving of oneself, this must also be true of all self-giving short of martyrdom. In the self one receives anew from God at every stage of self-expenditure, one is already becoming the self one will receive at the resurrection. Then it is not one life that one loses (mortal life lost in death) and another that one gains (eternal life in resurrection), but the same self that one is in self-giving one receives from God both now and eternally.

This key saying of Jesus (along with much that coheres with it in the New Testament and Christian tradition) therefore characterizes the way of the true self as one that is not a continuous line of maintaining one's self-identity, but a continually broken line, in that the true self lives in self-giving and self-denial. But as the self is continually given, so it is continually received afresh from God. This is life lived as gift of God. The self that knows itself to be given by God lives in giving itself, to and for God and others, and thus constantly receives itself as gift from God and from others. Here too it is God's grace that creates the continuity through the discontinuity. True self-identity is not found through maintaining it, but received through God's gift. This makes it intelligible that even through death, the final disruption of the narrative of the self, the continuity of the self is given by God. The false self that clings to life cannot survive death, but the true self that lives in self-abandonment to God receives itself again beyond death.

From the perspective of Christian theology it will seem extraordinary to have said so much without explaining its christological basis — that it is "in Christ" that Christians understand the true self to be found. But I have proceeded in this way for the sake of ease of exposition. Now that we have understood the two patterns of the narrative self — first, the loss of the false self and the finding of the true self, and second, the losing and finding of the true self — we can see how they are based in Jesus Christ and who he is for us.

Jesus lived and fulfilled his own saying, as the Gospels clearly indicate. In his self-expenditure in life and death he did not seek to preserve his life but gave it up for all of us. Losing it he found it in God's raising him from the dead. But Jesus is no mere example or paradigm of this pattern. Jesus is the one who gave his life for all of us, and so his resurrection is also for us all. As Jesus throughout his life received his life from God, never as a gift purely for himself, but always as life to be given for others, so his risen life, received from God beyond the absolute self-giving of his death, is given to him for others. The resurrection of Jesus is God's gift of Jesus' self to and for us.

Now we must see how the two patterns of the narrative self are given to us in Christ and realized for us in union with him. The key to this is the notion of loving identification, that is, the kind of love that is able to go out of itself in self-giving and truly to identify with others in their own situations and needs. It is through this kind of love that the true self transcends the self-enclosed concern of the false self, and finds itself in identification with others. It is this kind of love that binds us together with Christ in an identification initiated from his side and reciprocated from ours.

First, consider the loss of the false self and the finding of the true self. This is the place for Paul's claims that we have been crucified with Christ, as though our false selves were put to death when Jesus died on Golgotha. Jesus' self-giving for us entailed his loving identification with us in all the sinfulness of our false selves. His love could not truly reach us if it could not reach us in our false selves and liberate us from them. Thus our false selves were put to death in his death, and our true selves are given us in his risen life.

Second, consider the losing and finding of the true self. Finding our true selves in Christ, we identify with him who loved us, follow his way of self-giving for God and for others, and thus continually find ourselves afresh in him. The Christian self both gives and finds itself in the love of Jesus Christ.

CHAPTER 12

The Fulfillment of Messianic Prophecy

The subject of the Macbride University Sermon is described as "the application of the prophecies in Holy Scripture respecting the Messiah to our Lord and Saviour Jesus Christ." There have been times when Christians have attached great evidential value to the fulfillment by Jesus of Old Testament prophecies of the Messiah. They have wanted to argue not only that Jesus is shown to be the expected Messiah by the exact correspondences between the prophecies and their fulfillment in Jesus, but even that the fulfillment of these prophecies in Jesus is a kind of demonstration of the truth of Christianity. The fulfillment proves at the same time both that the prophecies were inspired by God and that Jesus was the Messiah that God himself sent. This kind of apologetic appeal to messianic prophecy is less often heard today. I think this must be at least partly due to the influence of biblical scholars who have insisted on a historicizing kind of exegesis that tries to read the prophecies as they would have been heard at the time they were written, and very often finds that this differs considerably from the way the writers of the New Testament read them when they interpreted them as referring to Jesus. I sense that New Testament scholars are sometimes a little embarrassed by the gap that seems to open between the historical meaning of the Old Testament texts and the way they were read by New Testament Christians. They explain in a matter-of-fact manner the way New Testament writers interpreted the Old, but they refrain from commenting on its validity.

But this is not a minor issue on which we can easily, as contemporary Christians, merely beg to differ from our first-century fathers and mothers in the faith. The identification of Jesus as the expected Messiah is after all what is meant by calling him Jesus Christ, "Christ" being simply the Greek translation of "Messiah." Christians are, literally, "messianists," people who consider Jesus to be the Messiah. Forgetting that Jesus is the Messiah goes along with a temptation that has been all too often influential in Christian history — the temptation to deny the essential Jewishness of Christian faith and to cut the New Testament's connection with the Old Testament. At stake in the issue of Jesus' messiahship is the whole question of the continuity between the two Testaments, the identity of the Christian God who is the God of Israel as well as the God of Jesus Christ and whose consistent purpose for the world was already made known to his people Israel, already set in motion through his people Israel, and reached a climactic stage in Jesus. For a whole raft of reasons Christians too easily imagine that God, as it were, started his project for the salvation of the world with Jesus. No, he started it with Abraham.

To make sense of Jesus' messiahship we really have to appreciate the way the early Christians read the whole Hebrew Bible as a book of dynamic expectation for the future, a book that, as it were, plots God's way to his coming kingdom of righteousness and peace in all the world. The passages we think of as messianic prophecies are those in which this orientation of the Old Testament to the messianic future becomes most obvious and explicit. But they are not detachable from the rest of the Old Testament. They have their roots in the long story of God's people, which the Old Testament tells; they express the same will of the same God who gave Israel the Torah; and the future they depict is shaped by the same concerns as the God of Israel characteristically expresses throughout the Old Testament — concerns for righteousness and peace, for the poor and the neglected, for Israel and for all the nations, even, we shall see, for the nonhuman creation. These concerns that God expresses in the Torah and seeks to implement in his dealings with his own people Israel seemed so often sadly ineffective but could never be abandoned, God being who God is. Throughout the Old Testament, in all its variety, they press forward, one way or another, toward God's coming kingdom. And often it is out of their apparent failure in the specific circumstances of Israel's story that they reach messianic expression, focused on a future that seems quite unattainable in human terms, but that must come because God is God and his purposes for the world cannot fail.

When we read the Old Testament that way, then I think we can see that a purely historicizing exegesis of messianic prophecies is not in fact adequate to their nature. They belong to the dynamic movement of the Old Testament toward the future. They are key expressions of that movement. We miss their real significance if we try to tie them down to the circumstances of their original composition. They are open texts whose meaning is not complete until the promises they make finally find fulfillment in reality. In many cases the editors of the Old Testament, who put together the actual collections of texts that we have, already — and surely quite deliberately — detached these prophecies from the original circumstances in which they were first composed. The prophecies had already left those circumstances behind in their drive toward the messianic future.

But here we perhaps run into another obstacle to Christian appreciation of the messianic prophecies. If these prophecies have been fulfilled in the New Testament's history of Jesus, then, while it may be interesting to observe that, do the prophecies any longer have anything to say to us? Doesn't the fulfillment supersede the prophecy? I think the answer is no: the prophecies continue to illuminate the reality of Jesus for us. This is really why the purely evidential use of messianic prophecy is inadequate. The New Testament writers do, indeed, cite the prophecies in order to show that Jesus fulfilled them, but they also turn to the prophecies to help them understand Jesus, to understand what God was really doing in the life, death, and resurrection of Jesus, to understand how it is that all the purposes of God for the world — purposes already known from the Hebrew Bible — are now focused in Jesus. Those purposes are not yet completed. Jesus himself as God's Messiah still has a future that is also the world's future. The messianic prophecies, read in a Christian way as referring to Jesus, still seek their fully adequate goal in the messianic kingdom to come.

So I do not think we should think of the messianic prophecies as exhausted, used up, superseded, with nothing to say to us. As indications of God's purpose for God's Messiah and the world they belong to the reality of Jesus. They and what the New Testament tells us of the historic reality of Jesus are mutually illuminating. Certainly we should read them in the light of Jesus' fulfillment of them, which was sometimes an unexpected or surprising kind of fulfillment that puts the prophecies in a new light. But we may also expect the prophecies to throw light for us on Jesus.

Now let's have done with generalities and consider one of the best known and extensive of the messianic prophecies: Isaiah 10:33–11:9. The Messiah here is the ideal ruler of the future, the new and better David, and we know this from Isaiah's use of the name Jesse, David's father. The Messiah is depicted as a shoot that grows out of the stump of Jesse, represented as a tree. The common habit of starting to read this passage at the beginning of chapter 11 deprives us of an important clue to the meaning of this image of the tree. The end of chapter 10 depicts God, with a great ax in his hand, hacking down a forest and felling the tallest trees. This is God executing judgment on the rulers and the powerful, those who arrogantly exalt themselves, usurping God's rule and using their power in flagrant disregard of God's righteousness. God hacks down the cedars of Lebanon, the Assyrian oppressors of Israel, but he also fells the tree of Jesse, the line of David's descendants, the royal house of David, the corrupt rulers of Israel and Judah. The Davidic monarchy has failed and God removes it. The stump of Jesse's tree is all that is left of the cherished promise of David and his successors for a kingdom of justice, compassion, and peace.

As so often, the hope of a Messiah rises from the ashes of disappointment for the coming of God's kingdom. The Messiah will not come from the failed dynasty of David. Rather God honors his promise to David in a quite unexpected way. He goes back to the origins of the dynasty, the root of Jesse's tree, and raises up a new shoot, as it were from nowhere, just as he had chosen David himself. Remember the story: David the youngest son of Jesse's eight, so insignificant that no one even thought to call him when Samuel was deciding which of Jesse's sons God had chosen for king. David the mere shepherd boy was God's surprising choice, though perhaps not so surprising when one gets to know the biblical God who characteristically chooses the least important, the least qualified in the eyes of the world. In David God hoped for a king after his own heart, a king who would not forget his origins among the humblest of his people, a king who would govern in compassionate solidarity with the poor.

So when David's royal descendants have got too used to the distancing privileges of power, God will make a fresh start, with a new David, a branch from the roots of Jesse. I think this image may help those of us who maybe have some difficulty with the pervasive image of kingship in the biblical messianic tradition. Neither the absolute rulers nor the constitutional monarchs we know seem to us to be very suitable models for the role the New Testament gives to Jesus. But the messianic king of the prophecies is not the regular sort of king, about whom the Bible itself is fairly derogatory. The messianic king is a sort of king that never was, a king from the people who never abandons his roots among the people, a king whose rule embodies God's concerns, a king who rules for the sake of all and therefore especially for the sake of the poor. Luke's portrayal of Jesus in the opening chapters of his Gospel echoes this messianic hope of the poor, not only in a way very familiar to us — the fact that shepherds are the first to be told of this new David — but also in a probably much less familiar way: in Luke's genealogy of Jesus' ancestry. It makes Jesus a descendant of David, certainly, but surprisingly not of Solomon and the famous kings of the Davidic dynasty; rather Jesus' ancestry derives from an obscure son of David, Nathan, and is traced through a host of quite unknown people (Luke 3:23-31). He is the shoot from the stump of Jesse.

Isaiah's picture of the Messiah and his rule unfolds around three themes that appear in succession: wisdom, justice, and peace. The wisdom comes from God: "The spirit of the LORD shall rest upon him, the spirit of wisdom and understanding, the spirit of counsel and might, the spirit of knowledge and the fear of the LORD" (Isa. 11:2). Out of this God-given wisdom comes the righteousness with which he rules, a righteousness that truly puts all wrongs to rights, and is therefore, as so often in the Old Testament, justice especially for those whose rights and interests are routinely disregarded, for those who have no one to lobby for them or means to work the system, the poor and the humiliated, the wretched of the earth. We begin to see how idealistically remote from experienced reality this messianic rule is. But there is more: "he shall strike the earth with the rod of his mouth and with the breath of his lips he shall kill the wicked" (Isa. 11:4). In other words, he has only to pronounce the just verdict for it to take effect. In this legal system violence is not needed to enforce the law. Nor is there the usual merely conventional correspondence of punishments with crimes. Rather, on this king's lips, truth itself is so undeniably true that it prevails by its own power.

And then there is peace, though Isaiah depicts it vividly without using that word. We must assume that there is peace between people: "They will not hurt or destroy in all my holy mountain" (11:9) must entail that. But the prophecy depicts peace unforgettably by focusing on the even less readily imaginable: peace in and with the world of animals. We are offered a kind of messianic ecology, a return to paradise perhaps, a frankly impossible world in which wild animals have changed their diets and their nature. But we should notice that the peace is not merely, as is usually observed, between predators and prey, but more specifically between wild animals and domesticated animals: wolf and lamb, lion and calf, bear and cow. What is reconciled is the human world and the world of wild nature. Strikingly, the only humans who actually appear in this picture are children: the little boy who leads the lion and the calf as though both were domestic animals, and the babies who play safely around the homes of snakes. The reason is surely the innocence and harmlessness of children. In this ideal world from which violence has been banished, those who are always the most unequivocally innocent victims of violence, the children, are finally safe. Just as when we think of justice we should especially remember the powerless whose rights are most easily neglected, so when we think of violence and war we should especially remember the children, the most innocent of victims.

This vision of the peaceable kingdom is evoked, I believe, in Mark's Gospel, when Jesus in the wilderness after his baptism is said to be "with the wild animals" (Mark 1:13). Jesus in his peaceable companionship with the wild animals symbolically, at least, establishes the messianic peace in all creation. This is a good illustration of the way the messianic prophecy still illuminates for us the messianic history, which we could not otherwise have understood in this way. And it also shows how the messianic prophecy still points the way of the messianic history into a future of adequate fulfillment — Jesus' own future with the world. I do not suggest we take Isaiah's picture literally, but I do suggest we take it seriously as pointing the way to God's final purpose of peace not only for humanity but for his whole creation.

It is a future that can only come from God. One last obstacle to Christian appreciation of the messianic prophecies I want to mention is the legacy in our thinking of the modern idea of progress. The goal of these prophecies, the kingdom of God, is no product of a process of historical progress. Not only is it historically implausible to assimilate this messianic hope to progress: are we any nearer to a reconciliation of humanity and wild nature than people were in Isaiah's day? Also, the vision here is certainly not processive or progressive; rather it makes a vast leap from the evil of the present to the inconceivable good of a quite discontinuous future. This is not a vision that grows out of the present, but one that breaks in from God's future.

And so how do we live with such a vision? I suggest that we live between messianic patience and messianic impatience. Knowing that this future can only come from God, we avoid the utopian impetus to establish a perfect world for ourselves, an impetus we know, not least from the history of the twentieth century, so often ends in violence and repression, devouring its own dream. We avoid too the paralyzing disappointment and disillusionment of failed utopianism. Messianic hope thrives in the desert of the humanly desperate. Its expectation looks to God. It waits patiently for God's time.

But equally we avoid the quietist withdrawal from history that simply leaves this world to its fate and finds consolation in a wholly otherworldly hope. We learn from Jesus the value of every anticipation of the messianic kingdom, large or small, limited but full of God's presence. Already the kingdom comes from God, in the fragmentary and fragile forms of historical existence. We do simply what we can, knowing that God can make much more of what we do than we can make of it ourselves. We welcome every anticipation of the kingdom with the messianic impatience that prays urgently "Your kingdom come."

So to confess Jesus the Messiah of this vision of Isaiah is to seek in Jesus the wisdom that comes of knowing God, to seek from Jesus the righteousness that puts all wrongs to rights, and to follow his way into the peaceable kingdom.

CHAPTER 13

Where Is Wisdom to Be Found?
Christ and Wisdom in Colossians

Colossians 1:15-20 is one of the most remarkable christological passages in the New Testament.[1] It is also one of the most problematic for theological appropriation today. In order to give some indication of the scope of the theological issues involved, I shall begin with the observation that in the theology of the last half century our passage has been prominent in three rather different respects:

First, there is the issue of the preexistence of Christ. Our passage was an important one for Karl Barth's argument that the preexistent Christ — the Christ who preexisted creation and was the one through whom and for whom all things were made, according to this Christ-hymn — should not be thought of as the *Logos asarkos,* the nonincarnate Logos, an abstract principle of cosmic order, but only as the man Jesus, the eternal Son of God already in God's intention the incarnate one.[2] Creation is through and for Jesus Christ. That means: God's covenant with humanity, established in the concrete form of Jesus of Nazareth, the one who is both God and human, is the basis of creation.[3] Barth was not denying but defining the

1. In its original publication, this essay accompanied and complemented an essay by Morna D. Hooker: "Where Is Wisdom to Be Found? Colossians 1.15-20 (1)," in *Reading Texts, Seeking Wisdom,* ed. David F. Ford and Graham Stanton (London: SCM, 2003) 116-28.

2. For discussion of this idea in Barth and Hendrikus Berkhof, see Chul Won Suh, *The Creation-Mediatorship of Jesus Christ,* Amsterdam Studies in Theology 4 (Amsterdam: Rodopi, 1982).

3. Karl Barth, *Church Dogmatics,* ed. T. F. Torrance and Geoffrey W. Bromiley (Edinburgh: T&T Clark, 1936-1969), II/2, pp. 94-102; Barth, *Church Dogmatics,* III/1, pp. 50-56. For criticism of this notion in Barth, see Wolfhart Pannenberg, *Systematic Theology,* trans. Geoffrey Bromiley (Grand Rapids: Eerdmans, 1994), 2:30, who takes Barth to mean only

personal preexistence of Christ, bringing it arguably closer to the way the Colossian Christ-hymn and similar New Testament passages speak of Jesus Christ himself as the subject of acts prior to his human existence.[4] But if Barth identified the preexistent subject of the hymn more closely with the man Jesus than traditional theology had done, other discussions of the Christology of this passage, such as those of James Dunn[5] and Karl-Josef Kuschel,[6] have done the opposite, reading the hymn as a poetic expression of the truth that God's action in Christ belongs to the same divine purpose as was expressed also in creation.

Second, our passage features prominently in the project of Walter Wink, in his three-volume work, *The Powers*,[7] to interpret and to explore the contemporary relevance of the New Testament, especially Pauline, language about the cosmic powers. Wink takes the powers to be not only angelic powers of the nonhuman world but also the inner spiritual dimension of the structures of human power. The Colossian Christ-hymn affirms their creation by God (they are not intrinsically evil), assumes their fall into that condition of hostility to God and to human flourishing that the rest of Colossians evidently assumes, and affirms also their reconciliation in Christ.[8] On this interpretation Wink builds an influential contemporary theology of Christian resistance to structural evil in human society that does not despair of the powers but works nonviolently, on the model of the cross, for their redemption.

"that it was with a view to the Son that the Father created us humans and our world," thereby neglecting "the Son's own subjectivity."

4. See Hans Urs von Balthasar, quoted in Walter A. Whitehouse, *The Authority of Grace: Essays in Response to Karl Barth*, ed. Ann Loades (Edinburgh: T&T Clark, 1981), p. 92: it is "exegetically impossible to understand [these passages] of an eternal divine Son or Logos *in abstracto*, but solely of him in his unity with the man Jesus."

5. James D. G. Dunn, *Christology in the Making* (London: SCM, 1980), pp. 187-94; Dunn, *The Epistles to the Colossians and to Philemon*, New International Greek Testament Commentary (Grand Rapids: Eerdmans, 1996), p. 89.

6. Karl-Josef Kuschel, *Born Before All Time? The Dispute over Christ's Origin*, trans. John Bowden (London: SCM, 1992), pp. 327-40, 491-96.

7. Walter Wink, *Naming the Powers: The Language of Power in the New Testament* (Philadelphia: Fortress, 1984); Wink, *Unmasking the Powers: The Invisible Forces That Determine Human Existence* (Philadelphia: Fortress, 1986); Wink, *Engaging the Powers: Discernment and Resistance in a World of Domination* (Minneapolis: Fortress, 1992).

8. For criticism of Wink's exegesis of Colossians, see Clinton E. Arnold, *Power and Magic: The Concept of Power in Ephesians*, 3rd ed. (Grand Rapids: Baker, 1997), pp. 47-51; Arnold, *The Colossian Syncretism: The Interface between Christianity and Folk Belief at Colossae* (Grand Rapids: Baker, 1996), pp. 267-68.

Third, the cosmic Christology of our passage has played an important part in attempts to retrieve and to develop a theology of creation relevant to the ecological crisis resulting from modern humanity's destructive relationship to the rest of God's creation. In this role the Colossian Christ-hymn already featured centrally in the pioneering ecological theology of Joseph Sittler[9] and remains important in more recent endeavors, such as that of Jürgen Moltmann.[10] Whereas other parts of Scripture affirm the value of all creatures as God's creation, the Colossian Christ-hymn goes further in bringing the whole creation within the central concern of the Christian gospel: salvation in Christ.[11] It relates Christ himself not only to redemption but also to creation; it relates creation to redemption; and it extends the scope of reconciliation through Christ as far as the whole creation. It seems an appropriate biblical basis for overcoming the anthropological restriction of so much of the theology of the modern period. On the other hand, we might note that Celia Deane-Drummond in a recent book called *Creation through Wisdom* protests against the restriction of cosmic Wisdom to Christology that too exclusive a reliance on this passage entails.[12]

These have been the three, rather separate lines of theological interest in our passage in theology from Barth to the present. But do they have any bearing on the question: Where is wisdom to be found? We should recall that the meaning of wisdom, that is, God's wisdom, in the Jewish theological tradition to which our passage belongs has to do with the created order of things and with the divine purpose for creation. It is God's wisdom that orders creation for its well-being, God's wisdom that can be perceived in the good order of the natural creation, God's wisdom that ordains good

9. Joseph Sittler, *Evocations of Grace: The Writings of Joseph Sittler on Ecology, Theology, and Ethics,* ed. Steven Bouma-Prediger and Peter Bakken (Grand Rapids: Eerdmans, 2000), especially pp. 30-31, 38-50 (this reflection on Col. 1:15-20 was first published in 1962), 105-12 (first published in 1972).

10. Jürgen Moltmann, *The Way of Jesus Christ,* trans. Margaret Kohl (London: SCM, 1990), pp. 276-86, 304-7, 312. On cosmic Christology in Sittler and Moltmann, see Steven Bouma-Prediger, *The Greening of Theology: The Ecological Models of Rosemary Radford Ruether, Joseph Sittler, and Jürgen Moltmann* (Atlanta: Scholars Press, 1995).

11. Some relationship between redemption by Christ and the whole creation is also suggested by Phil. 2:10 and Rev. 5:13.

12. Celia E. Deane-Drummond, *Creation through Wisdom: Theology and the New Biology* (Edinburgh: T&T Clark, 2000), chap. 4 and pp. 236-41; cf. Deane-Drummond, "Futurenatural? A Future of Science through the Lens of Wisdom," *Heythrop Journal* 40 (1999): 47-51.

ways of human living in the world, and God's wisdom that, beyond the disruption of creation's good by evil, purposes the ultimate well-being, the *shalom,* the peace of the whole creation. According to Colossians, this wisdom of God is all to be found in Jesus Christ (see 2:3). Whatever else we might make of this claim, it is not that Jesus Christ is one among many expressions of the creative and redemptive wisdom of God. It is that Jesus Christ is that wisdom. When we recognize both the scope of wisdom in this passage, encompassing all creation, its origin and goal, and also its christological concentration, such that the reconciliation of all things occurs through the cross of Jesus, it is surely clear that at least all three of the lines of theological interest in this passage I have noted would be needed to do theological justice to it and to answer the question: Where is wisdom to be found? Wisdom is found in the whole creation, and it is found in the crucified and risen Jesus, and somehow these two are the same.

The following are my own theological reflections on the issue:

(1) The relevance and appeal of the Colossian Christ-hymn today may well lie in the holistic character of its depiction of the wise purposes of God. It clearly surmounts the false dualisms that have too often marred the Christian worldview. By false dualisms I mean the privileging of one aspect of reality at the expense of its correlate — for example, the dualisms of nature and history, the spatial and the temporal, matter and spirit, the nonhuman and the human, creation and salvation, the order of creation and the eschatological. These dualisms of reality also relate to the contrasts, often set up as exclusive, between such biblical traditions as wisdom and salvation history or wisdom and apocalyptic, and of course also to such theological polarities as natural theology and theology of the cross. In some sense the Colossian Christ-hymn invites us to see the world whole, and there is much in our cultural climate that makes that congenial.

(2) What may be less culturally congenial is that the holism of our passage is christological. Dualism is overcome or (better) avoided because Jesus Christ is both the firstborn of the whole creation and the firstborn from the dead, because those remarkably significant prepositional phrases "through him" and "for him" are so strikingly applied both to the creation of all things and to the reconciliation of all things. This christological coherence of all things is best appreciated, in my view, when we recognize the passage as an expression of what Tom Wright[13] and I have both called the

---

13. N. T. Wright, *The Climax of the Covenant: Christ and the Law in Pauline Theology* (Edinburgh: T&T Clark, 1991), pp. 114-19.

christological monotheism of the New Testament writings. In the terms I have advocated elsewhere,[14] what the passage does is to include Jesus Christ in God's unique relationship to the whole of created reality and thereby to include Jesus in the unique identity of God as Jewish monotheism understood it.

There are two especially strong indications of this. One is the sixfold occurrence of the phrase "all things" and the twofold reference to the heavens and the earth: these universal references are ubiquitous in the rhetoric of Jewish monotheism. They specify the unique relationship in which God stands to the whole of created reality, as Creator of all things and Lord over all things. Especially striking is the inclusion of Jesus in God's relationship as Creator to all things. It was creation that most unambiguously marked the absolute distinction between God and all other reality. It was emphatically denied that in the work of creation God was assisted by anyone else, though this was quite compatible with saying that God created by his word or his wisdom, since these were not "someone else" but God's own word and wisdom, intrinsic to his identity. Second, the unique relationship of God to the whole creation was sometimes specified by prepositional phrases indicating three of the forms of causation recognized in ancient philosophy: all things were created by God (efficient causation), through God (instrumental causation), and for God (final causation).[15] It is therefore in God's relationship to the world that the Colossian hymn includes Jesus Christ when it makes him both the instrumental and the final cause of both the creation and the reconciliation of all things: "through him" and "for him." Finally, it is important that both these features of monotheistic rhetoric occur, in close parallelism, in both stanzas of the hymn, referring both to creation and to reconciliation. The two stanzas concern the same one God's relationship to his world and include Jesus in this uniquely divine relationship to all things in the same way in both cases.

Thus it is christological monotheism that makes it possible to view the world whole in the way that the Colossian hymn does. The original and restored unity of all things could not be found in Christ if Christ did not share the uniquely divine relationship of the one God to all things.

(3) For all the emphatic universality of the whole hymn, there is

---

14. Richard Bauckham, *God Crucified: Monotheism and Christology in the New Testament* (Grand Rapids: Eerdmans, 1999).

15. See the examples in James D. G. Dunn, *Romans 9–16*, Word Biblical Commentary 38B (Dallas: Word, 1988), pp. 701-2.

also no missing the intense particularity of the man Jesus indicated by the phrase "the blood of his cross" (1:20). Combination of particularity and universality — the particular identity of Jesus and the universal relevance or effect of his history — is characteristic of New Testament Christology. But whereas in most cases there is a movement from the particularity of Jesus to the eschatological universality of his future, in the Colossian hymn this is also grounded in the prior universality of his relationship to creation. The effect, as far as I can see, is not at all to reduce the significance of the particularity of the man Jesus, relativizing him by reference to a Christ who is bigger than Jesus (a phrase of John Robinson's[16]), but, on the contrary, to reinforce the universal relevance of precisely the man Jesus. To see the world whole we must see it in relationship to the crucified and risen Jesus, for whom all things were created.

(4) What then is the meaning of the hymn's implicit claim that all the wisdom of God is to be found in Christ? The implicit claim is explicit elsewhere in Colossians in the statement that in Christ "are hidden all the treasuries of wisdom and knowledge" (2:3). The author of one book on Colossians, Richard DeMaris, accuses the writer of denigrating the cosmos, locating "God's wisdom narrowly, entirely in Christ (Col 1:26; 2:2-4), to the apparent exclusion of all else (2:8, 20)."[17] But the cosmic Christ of the Colossian Christ-hymn is not narrow; he is all-encompassing. The effect is not to denigrate wisdom wherever it may be found, but to claim it for Christ, in other words to claim that only from the vantage point of the crucified and risen Jesus can creation, in all the ways in which it reflects the wisdom of its Creator, be seen whole.[18] The reason is the intrusion of evil that takes place implicitly between the first and second stanzas of the hymn. (Colossians is as reticent about the origins of evil as most of the Bible is.) In this disordered state of God's creation the perception and affirmation of his wise ordering of creation requires faith in his purpose,

16. John A. T. Robinson, *The Human Face of God* (London: SCM, 1973), p. 10: "the Christ is bigger than Jesus."

17. Richard E. DeMaris, *The Colossian Controversy: Wisdom in Dispute at Colossae,* Journal for the Study of the New Testament Supplement Series 96 (Sheffield: Sheffield Academic, 1994), p. 149.

18. Cf. Colin Gunton, "Christ, the Wisdom of God: A Study in Divine and Human Action," in *Where Shall Wisdom Be Found? Wisdom in the Bible, the Church and the Contemporary World,* ed. S. C. Barton (Edinburgh: T&T Clark, 1999), p. 260: "To say that the crucified Christ is the Wisdom of God is to say that he is the key to the meaning of the whole of the created order, and therefore the source of true wisdom, wherever that is to be found."

revealed and established in Jesus Christ, to make it whole. This purpose is hidden because the event that establishes it looks for all the world like a triumph for the forces of violence and disorder that ravage creation. Hidden in the crucified and risen Christ is the secret of God's purpose for all things that puts in true perspective all traces of his wisdom in the whole creation.

(5) The most difficult aspect of the Christ-hymn for a contemporary hermeneutical appropriation seems to me the notion of cosmic reconciliation. But since this aspect also holds out considerable promise of speaking to our situation of ecological destruction, it may be worth persisting with the difficulty. I am not as troubled as many commentators by the apparent contradiction between the reconciliation of all things, presumably including the powers, in the hymn (1:19-20), and Christ's triumph over the powers, depicted later in 2:15. Both images are of pacification, but since both are *images* I do not see that they need be compatible in literal terms. Since we barely know what the powers are, I do not think we need expect to know, in literal terms, how they are pacified by Christ.

I find the notion of the reconciliation of all things problematic in two other ways. The first is the issue of what there is about the nonhuman creation that needs reconciliation. Science seems to reveal a world in which the interplay of order and chaos is so intimate that it is very hard to disentangle a good order that would be better for the overcoming of disorder. To put it crudely, the lion that lay down with the lamb would starve. Perhaps we may be content to leave that issue in the mystery of God's purpose and to focus — as surely the most relevant aspect of the matter for our contemporary context — on the disorder wrought by the exercise of human power in creation. This idea of humanly produced disorder in creation is not at all difficult to understand, and its evidence is all around us.

The second problem I have is with the apparent anthropocentricity of the picture. The notion of cosmic redemption certainly breaks out of the anthropological restriction of too much Christian theology and encompasses the whole of the creation. But if it takes the blood of the incarnate Christ, of the man Jesus, to redeem the nonhuman world, does this not presuppose an anthropocentric creation? Perhaps we could say that it presupposes not anthropocentricity in a general sense and certainly not that the rest of creation exists for humanity's sake, but rather the distinctive place that humanity occupies in the world. This distinctiveness is evident in the brute fact of the power we have to affect and to damage the rest of nature. We might connect this also with supposing that it is especially in human society that the powers of evil are able to influence the world for ill. Cosmic reconciliation is focused in the human person of Jesus because it is humanity that constitutes at least the core of the problem for the rest of creation as well as for ourselves. The power of supra-human forces of evil is overcome within human history because it is there that they have gained their most significant hold in creation.

If this makes cosmic redemption anthropocentric, it does so in a very different way from the arrogant progressivism of the modern era, for which human domination of the rest of nature seemed the path of salvation and the humanization of the cosmos its God-given destiny.[19] What prevents the assimilation of the Colossian Christ-hymn to any such progressivist vision of the world is its stubborn reminder of the particularity of Jesus: "the blood of his cross." That recognition of the chaos and evil at the heart of human history requires us to relate to the rest of God's creation in humility and trust, with love rather than with mastery, in search of the peace that is the well-being of all creatures, not the well-being of ourselves at the expense of all others. That is one of the paths along which wisdom is to be found.

19. The classic expression of this view in christological form is that of Pierre Teilhard de Chardin. Cf. Whitehouse, *Authority,* pp. 95-96, where, having raised, as an obstacle for the modern mind to belief in the cosmic role of Christ, its "anthropocentric character," he attempts to remove the obstacle thus: "The history of nature is coming under man's dominion to an increasing degree; it is being increasingly permeated by man's purposes; and the effect is not wholly detrimental. Is not this a token, however ambiguous or proleptic, that it is already permeated by the mind and will which received historical expression in the man Jesus Christ? The mind and will by which mankind tends to permeate the cosmos independently must of course be transformed if they are to become the mind and will of Christ. But signs of this transformation are not altogether lacking in the changing pattern of man's thought and purposes." In the light of the ecological crisis, such statements must be subject to a hermeneutic of suspicion. They are theological justifications of the modern project of human domination of nature.

CHAPTER 14

What Is Truth?

When I was invited to speak about truth, my thoughts went, in one direction, to the Gospel of John, because, although truth is a frequent topic in the New Testament, use of the words "true" and "truth" is especially characteristic of that Gospel. So I have structured what I have to say around a number of aspects of truth as they appear in John's Gospel. But my thoughts also went, in another direction, to the contest about truth that is going on in our contemporary Western culture. This is a contest in which what are now known as modern and postmodern attitudes to truth contend. It should also be a context with which Christian truth must engage in a way that is identical with neither a modern nor a postmodern approach but seeks an authentically Christian way.

(1) Postmodern Pilate

" 'What is truth?' said jesting Pilate, and did not stay for an answer." These often quoted words of Francis Bacon allude of course to the account of Jesus' trial before Pilate in John's Gospel. In fact, it is with the question "What is truth?" that Pilate brings that trial, such as it was, to an end (John 18:38). It is not a genuine question, but a way of exiting the conversation, which Jesus had brought round to the matter of truth. Its tone is dismissive. The pragmatic politician thus prepares the way for his cynical surrender to the death of a man he knows to be innocent.

Pilate's nonquestion is, I think we can fairly say, a postmodern one, that is, it is a question characteristic of our times. Has truth ever seemed such a dubious notion as it does for many in our society? There are a number of reasons, including these: (1) The unprecedented pluralism of our contemporary Western societies suggests to many that truth must be relative, if anything. Rival truth claims provoke skepticism about all truth claims. (2) The unprecedented individualism of our contemporary Western societies makes individuals feel autonomous and so not bound to any tradition of religion or ideas. If the individual feels free to choose their own truths in the consumerist marketplace of ideas the sense of truth as there to be acknowledged or discovered too easily gives way to a sense that truth is subject to my freedom. It's not truth that obliges my acknowledgment of it, but my choice, my taste, my convenience that determines truth. Truth is what works for me, and therefore not necessarily what will work for you.

These relativizing, even individualizing approaches to truth claims have as their corollary a suspicion of all claims to universal truth. Big claims to truth look like attempts to foist my truth onto you. And the suspicion goes further: attempts to propagate allegedly universal truth are instruments of power, ways of suppressing difference. From the disillusioned perspective of postmodern people all truth is just a vehicle of the human will to power.

So postmodernity has problematized truth. Not that it was ever an uncontroversial subject, as Pilate's question again reminds us. But those are, as it were, the contours of the problem of truth in our time and place. I shall sketch the contours a little more as I proceed. But I want at once to point out that Western society is both modern and postmodern. That is to say, currents of postmodern thinking coexist with by no means exhausted modern attitudes. An example is science. While postmodern thinkers do apply their corrosive suspicion of all truth claims to science also, and while alternative therapies, for example, have relativized for many people the universal claims of orthodox medical science, nevertheless science retains a prestige in our societies as the only sort of truth that seems to stand up without relativizing or individualizing. One might have thought the "science has disproved religion" sort of argument would have gone the way of other kinds of modernist rationalism, but in the United Kingdom at least it is alive and well.

(2) Truth in Person

Pilate's question did not expect an answer, but the reader of John's Gospel knows its true answer. Jesus himself is the truth. "I am the way, the truth, and the life," he has said four chapters earlier (14:6). The pity is that the answer to Pilate's question stood there before him, but in the act of asking the question Pilate turns away from him.

But what can it mean to say that Jesus is the truth? Not just that he speaks the truth, though he does. More than that, he embodies the truth in the way he lives and dies and is raised from death. He is the key to all truth, the one in whom God reveals to us as much as we can know of the ultimate truth of things.

Notice, then, three implications for the kind of truth in which the Christian gospel deals: First, truth in John's Gospel, truth in the sense that Jesus is truth, is a rich, multidimensional, holistic concept. It refers not just to a number of true statements, but to a whole way of living and dying. We shall come back to that. Second, truth is found in encounter. In all genuine discovery of truth there is the sense of encountering something real, coming up against something we must acknowledge and recognize. We are ourselves in the encounter, of course; we put ourselves into it; it has a subjective element. But we also come up against something that has its own reality and integrity. In the genuine encounter with reality we cannot grasp and possess it, get it into our own control, direct it to our own ends. In that kind of attempt to take over truth and to use it, we retreat from encounter and distort the truth. In encounter truth cannot be fully grasped; there is always more to it than we have seen, but for all that our partial perception is a genuine sighting of reality.

That truth is encountered we see most fully in the case of Jesus as truth. As the human person he is, as God embodied in a human life, his personal reality confronts us. He eludes our grasp, as all persons do in genuinely personal encounter. We cannot apply to him the modern rationalist desire to master truth, but nor is the postmodern notion of constructing our own truth for ourselves appropriate — not, once again, if we encounter him in his personal otherness. Of course, it is in fact all too easy to construct a Jesus figure of our own making — Jesus as we would like him to be, a Jesus who is nothing but a reflection of ourselves or our ideals, even a Jesus as we fear he may be. Quests of the historical Jesus — modern or postmodern — always run that risk. But when they fall for it they evade the experience of encounter, preferring a useful idol to the personal otherness of Jesus. They turn, like Pilate, from the possibility of encounter back to mastery and control.

Third, Jesus was and is a particular human person, as well as being the universal God. His story in the Gospels is a very particular bit of human history. Yet he is, Christians have always believed, of universal relevance.

Thus truth, in this case as throughout Scripture, is both particular and universal, and universal only by being particular. God makes himself particular in order to be God for all people.

This very characteristic combination of the particular and the universal is where Christian truth distinguishes itself from both modern and postmodern ways. Conversely, the modernist and the postmodernist object to it for precisely opposite reasons. For the modernist truth is universal and must be universally evident to human reason. Truth has to be something like mathematics, which is simply true at any time and place. Truth, in the important sense of truth to live by, cannot be particular. No particular person could embody the universal truth of God.

For the postmodernist, on the other hand, there is only the particular. The Enlightenment's supposedly universal truths were merely the ideas of Western culture imposed by a kind of cultural imperialism on other people. The only truths are particular. There is my truth or our group's truth, but it cannot be exported.

For Christians, truth is accessible in the particular story and person of Jesus. But it is not just our truth. In the particular story and person of Jesus truth is accessible to all people. This is the experience of those who have encountered truth in Jesus across a huge diversity of cultures, times, and places. To be sure, their experience was contextual. That is, they encountered Jesus from within the contextual reality of their cultures, times, and places. The ways in which the universal relevance of Jesus came home to them in particular differed. The truth of God in Jesus is big enough to relate to all human contexts in their particularity as well as in the common human condition they all share. But it was the universal relevance of the particular human being whose story they read in the Gospels that they have encountered — and still do. Does this account of the universality of Jesus actually mask some kind of Christian authoritarianism and oppression? We shall come back to that.

(3) Practicing Truth

The Gospel of John speaks not only of believing the truth but also of doing the truth: "all who do evil hate the light and do not come to the light, so that their deeds may not be exposed. But those who do what is true come to the light, so that it may be clearly seen that their deeds have been done in God" (3:20-21).

This is another insight into the holistic nature of truth as this Gospel expounds it. This is a truth that in the end we cannot know without practicing it. That "doing the truth" seems to us an odd phrase may be a symptom of a rather too narrowly intellectual idea of truth. But if Jesus embodies truth, then truth requires us also to embody it in our lives. If the story of Jesus is a true story in the profound sense that in it we encounter the truth of God, then our own stories must in some sense reflect his. Our own stories need to be true stories too.

Jesus also says (in fact, these are the words of Jesus to which Pilate's dismissive response is his nonquestion "What is truth?"): "Everyone who belongs to the truth listens to my voice" (18:37). Like "doing the truth," this also sounds rather unfamiliar and odd. We should attend rather carefully to those parts of Scripture that sound a little odd (or a lot odd), since the oddness suggests there may be something we have to learn. "Everyone who belongs to the truth" — notice how at a stroke Jesus contradicts any propensity we have to think truth belongs to us. This is no "truth for me." Nor is it truth we can grasp and use for ourselves, and we dare not impose it on others as though it were ours to impose. The Gospel does not belong to Christians. It belongs to Jesus and we belong to it. It claims us and requires us to listen.

To belong to truth is to listen to Jesus, to speak truth, and to do truth.

(4) Authoritative Truth

Jesus in the Gospel of John underlines the truth of some of his most important sayings by beginning them, "Truly, truly, I say to you . . ." (This formula occurs twenty-five times in the Gospel.) Literally, the phrase is "Amen, amen, I say to you . . ." The word "amen" derives from the Hebrew word for "truth." The point of saying "Amen" at the end of a prayer is to underline our agreement with the prayer, making it our own prayer. "Yes, yes," we mean. "Yes, it's true." When people in a Pentecostal congregation shout out "Amen" in response to something the preacher has said, they are using the term quite correctly. But Jesus says it not in response but in introduction. It underlines the authority with which he speaks: "This is really the truth, you must believe it."

Does that not sound authoritarian? It is revealing to notice that, whereas *authority* used to be a good word, distinguished from *authoritarianism,* which was a misuse or distortion of authority, many people in our contemporary culture make no such distinction. Authority is oppressive because it seems to contradict freedom. And freedom is the overriding value of contemporary Western society.

In Philip Pullman's fantasy trilogy *His Dark Materials,* God is usually referred to as "the Authority." The term has entirely negative connotations. God's representatives on earth, ecclesiastical institutions, seem to be responsible for all the oppression against which good human instincts rebel. The plot reruns the story of Satan's failed rebellion against God in *Paradise Lost.* This time Eve and Adam eat of the tree with impunity and the forces of rebellion overthrow the Authority forever. The authoritarian kingdom of heaven, Pullman hopes, will give way to a republic of heaven.

It is a brilliant, mythological version of the modernist secular story of human freedom heroically won from the oppressive authoritarianism of traditional religion. It is a peculiarly appealing story in our time. Is there an alternative Christian story — a story of authoritative truth that so far from suppressing freedom enables true freedom? Jesus evidently thought so, for he also says in John's Gospel, "The truth will set you free" (8:32).

(5) Liberating Truth

The full sentence is this: "If you continue in my word, you are truly my disciples, and you will know the truth, and the truth will set you free" (8:31-32). Here the truth that sets free is found in discipleship of Jesus. Here is a freedom that is not the total autonomy of the individual, not freedom from everything and mastery over everything, but a freedom found in belonging and consistent even with obedience. How can this be? How can God's truth be authoritative without being authoritarian?

Let's recall the broad context in which Jesus says this: the Gospel story. It's the story of God's love for the world, love such that his Son came to die for the world. To return to Pilate — we noticed the irony of the fact that it was when God's truth incarnate stood before him that Pilate turned away with his skeptical "What is truth?" But the irony goes further. Pilate's dismissal of truth sends Jesus to the cross, and this, the paradoxical climax of John's story, is where above all Jesus enacts God's truth. Jesus is no less and never more the embodiment of the truth of things — the reality of God's love for the world — than when he dies on the cross.

So the authority with which Jesus speaks and acts, the authority of God's truth in this story, is the authority of grace. Through Jesus Christ,

John's Prologue tells us, grace and truth happened (1:17). This category — the authority of grace — is a key category in the biblical understanding of authority that distinguishes it radically from any kind of authoritarian domination. The biblical story is not, as Philip Pullman would have it, a story of domination, coerced obedience, and rebellious autonomy, but a story of God's grace (his loving giving) and our free and glad response. In this story all is given by God, including freedom. The world, our being in it, our redemption from the evil we make of it — all are God's gift, and in God's dealings with us gift always precedes God's requirements of us.

We noticed that real truth is demanding: it claims us and requires us to live according to it. But before it is demanding it is, just as characteristically, gracious and liberating. To the truth of God's love for us our response is not the coerced submission of the slave, but the free obedience of love. Its paradigm is that verse of Psalm 40 in which the early Christians heard Jesus speaking: "I delight to do your will, O my God; your law is within my heart" (Ps. 40:8; cf. Heb. 10:7). This is the obedience of those who glimpse the possibility of their best desires converging with God's, who recognize God's will as the desire of their own hearts, whose experience of God's love makes love the freely chosen goal of their lives.

Because obedience to God, whose will is the true law of my own being, is different in kind from obedience to any human authority, the biblical writers struggle with analogies for it. The analogy of servants' or slaves' obedience to their masters or subjects' obedience to their king is frequent, but also transmuted by paradox: "As slaves of God live as free people," says Peter (1 Pet. 2:16), while James speaks of obeying "the perfect law, the law of freedom" (1:25). In John's Gospel, in Jesus' long farewell to the disciples, he says: "You are my friends if you do what I command you. I do not call you servants any longer, because the servant does not know what the master is doing; but I have called you friends, because I have made known to you everything I have heard from my Father" (15:14-15). What Jesus drops there from the image of servant is not the language of command and obedience, but the requirement of blind obedience that is made of the mere slave. Like Jesus himself in obedience to his Father, his friends know the aim his commandments have in view, and themselves endorse and conform to that aim.

Let me illustrate, in a limited but contemporary fashion, one way in which accepting the authoritative truth of the gospel can be liberating. We live in a society that exalts postmodern autonomy with its supposed freedom of the individual to choose in every area of life. But this postmodern freedom is not all it's cracked up to be. Most postmodern people are strongly constrained by cultural trends, the media, the commercial interests that promote advertising and fashion, peer expectations, and so on. Those whom this consumerist culture supposedly sets free are as often as not subject to compulsions to work excessively and to conform to impossibly demanding expectations of success (levels of stress have never been higher) or alternatively to the compulsions of drug abuse and the empty quest for fulfillment in merely hedonistic pleasure. Choices are indeed multiplied to an unprecedented extent, but many of them are merely trivial. Really significant choices are much more difficult to find in a society that values choice as such, rather than the ability to make good as opposed to bad choices. Misled by the postmodern message that any value is as good as any other, people make ignorantly disastrous choices and suffer uncomprehendingly from them.

People who become Christians may well find it a liberation from all of that. To put oneself under the authority of God is a way of breaking with the cultural pressure, the demands of other people's opinions and expectations, the interiorized demands of the advertisers, the need to get on and to get ahead. It is a way of making for once a thoroughly nontrivial choice about the whole way one sees and lives life. It is a way into a world in which there are real values to guide one and real truth to conform to. It may be demanding, but unlike the irrational compulsions of consumerism and hedonism, it has a truly desirable goal in view.

How sad, then, it is to see Christians themselves entangled in the enslaving pseudo-freedoms of consumerism. What Paul said to the foolish Galatians applies: "For freedom Christ has set us free. Stand firm, therefore, and do not submit again to a yoke of slavery" (5:1).

(6) "His Testimony Is True"

If the truth of God, the true revelation of the reality of things, is to be found in Jesus and his story, how can we know it? In the way the Gospel of John sees this, a key category is that of testimony, or witness to the truth. The Gospel itself claims to be the testimony of the Beloved Disciple, that anonymous disciple of Jesus who appears rather unobtrusively in the Gospel narrative until he finally emerges as one specially qualified to witness not only to what happened but also to its significance. His "testimony is true" (a remark made twice in the Gospel: 19:35; 21:24) both because he was there and because he was given the insight of a truly competent witness to events of such history-making significance.

In my book *Jesus and the Eyewitnesses* I have explored the notion of eyewitness testimony in relation to the Gospels.[1] It is a mistake to suppose that we can dig behind the Gospels historically and reconstruct a purely historical Jesus who could be of any significance or interest for faith. Like most historical evidence, what we have in the Gospels is testimony, and it is the kind of testimony ancient historians most valued: the testimony of involved participants who spoke of the meaning of events they experienced from the inside. Dispassionate observers are not the best sources for much of what we want to know about history. Especially with uniquely significant, history-making events, where crude ideas of uniformity in history break down, we need testimony from the inside. The Holocaust is the signal modern example of an event we should have no real conception of without the testimony of survivors.

If we want to know anything significant about Jesus, we must trust the testimony of the eyewitnesses that we have in the Gospels. Trusting testimony is a normal, perfectly rational thing to do. We do it all the time in daily life: that is, we believe people who are in a position to know what they tell us, unless we have reason not to trust them. One can try to test the reliability of witnesses — we don't have to believe them uncritically or gullibly — but if we do find them reliable then they have to be trusted. We cannot independently verify everything they say. That's the point of testimony. So while I am not trying to dispense with faith in the special sense of faith in God and in Jesus or to deny that such faith is response to the disclosure of God in the Gospel history, I do think that historiographical and theological considerations converge in the nature of the Gospels. The Gospels do not require us to tear faith and history apart, but invite us to find them consistent.

Those who were eyewitnesses of the Gospel events are unique in the kind of witness to Jesus they bear. Without their witness no one else could be followers of Jesus. And this is why John's Gospel, though it is often misunderstood at this point, confines the language of witness and testimony to the immediate disciples of Jesus who, like the Beloved Disciple, told what they saw. "You also," says Jesus to them, "are to testify, because you have been with me from the beginning" (15:27). That cannot be said of any but

---

1. Richard Bauckham, *Jesus and the Eyewitnesses: The Gospels as Eyewitness Testimony* (Grand Rapids: Eerdmans, 2006).

the original disciples of Jesus. The reason for this limitation is, of course, that the truth to which they witness *happened* in history. The gospel is not a matter of timeless truths or good ideas or moral injunctions, but the story of God's grace happening in the world in the events of Jesus' life, ministry, death, and resurrection. Jesus as he is in that Gospel story is the truth. So the witnesses have to have been there. As John's Gospel says of the Beloved Disciple at the cross: "He who saw this has testified" (19:35).

That is what John wishes to stress, but it need not rule out the use of the word *witness,* as by some other New Testament writers, as a calling of all Christians and of the Christian church throughout history. We simply need to be clear about the difference between the eyewitnesses and ourselves — otherwise we shall neglect the historical truth of the Gospel, its happened-ness — but then we may also call the church's testimony to the truth testimony in a secondary form.

(7) The Truth of Testimony

The way that Christians tell the truth is by way of witness. This is so because of the nature of the truth to which they witness. I want to stress and to dwell on this point a little because it relates to the widespread current criticism of religions that claim universal truth. I have already cited the postmodern point that such claims are authoritarian, mask oppression, and delegitimize difference. But the point is even more strongly made in the idea that religions that make universal claims incite and sanction violence. The current popularity of this view — at least in the United Kingdom — is connected with the surprising resurgence of religion as a hugely effective force in the world. Surprising to secularists, that is, because they had expected the steady decline of religion. Instead, we see radical Islamists determined to change the world through self-sacrificial violence. (Clearly this is not something else disguised as religion because suicide bombing is incomprehensible without religious motivation.) At the time of the Iraq war, some people also saw right-wing American fundamentalism driving an American and British attempt to impose Western values on Islamic countries by force and violence. A clash of violent ideologies? This would be too simple an analysis, but one can easily appreciate how those who abhor such violence put it in succession to the religiously sanctioned violence of the past, such as the Inquisition and the Crusades. Isn't such violence necessarily produced by religions committed to absolute truths that require acceptance by all people? Isn't there a kind of violence already in the intolerant assertion that we have the truth and others who differ from us do not?

In response we should make it entirely clear that assent to any claims to truth may not be enforced. Truth loses its own power to convince when we suppose it needs law enforcement and violence to secure its place in the world. Coercion of any kind — and there are forms of coercion other than the purely physical — is what distorts truth into a vehicle for the will to power. There are certainly few more oppressive regimes than those that believe they stand for a truth that must be enforced (though such a truth need not be religious). Christianity has always known in principle that belief cannot be coerced, though in practice all too often Christians have endorsed the religious use of coercion. That is why we need to be so clear and resolute about this. Christian truth cannot be coerced. *It ceases to be true if it is.*

Any kind of truth claim has its own appropriate way of inviting belief. Scientific truth, for example, has its own means of claim and methods of verification. They are appropriate to science, but we should not suppose that the success of science makes the same means and methods normative for other kinds of truth. Probably the best way of describing the way in which Christian truth should be claimed is the image of witness. Witness is noncoercive. It can be compelling but it cannot be compulsory. That is, its power to convince resides in the truth to which it witnesses, not in the power of those who witness. Often enough, as in the cases of the cross and the martyrs, the powerlessness of the witnesses is the vehicle of the truth's power to convince.

Adequate witness to the truth of God in Jesus Christ must be holistic. As we have seen, this is truth that cannot be known without also being practiced. Witness to it must involve the whole of life and even death. Only then can one see that the witness is not self-serving, not manipulative, but transparent to the truth to which it points.

In the current concern about religious violence people commonly claim that it's religious "extremists" (one of the meanings given to that slippery term *fundamentalists*) that are the problem. People who are moderate about their religion are okay, it is implied. It is when people take their religion too seriously that they begin to threaten the rest of us. The trouble with an Al-Qaeda suicide bomber is that he really believes that his cause is worth dying for and he is assured of paradise if he gives everything for it.

I do not buy that approach. There is nothing moderate about loving

God with all our heart and all our soul, all our mind and all our strength — as the God of Israel demanded and Jesus heartily endorsed. There was nothing moderate about Mother Teresa or Dietrich Bonhoeffer or any of those people Christians have recognized as saints. Mother Teresa surely was a religious extremist, extreme in her love of God and her devotion to the poor, extreme in giving up so much and giving herself so much to others. Sanctity is extreme, and it is, I think, significant that, while secularism may produce outstandingly moral people, only religion produces saints.

So we should not be seduced by the secular desire to keep religion within comfortable bounds, even though violent and coercive forms of religious adherence make such a desire understandable. Not the whole-hearted commitment to truth is the problem, but the kind of truth that is at stake. The truth of God in Jesus Christ demands wholehearted commitment to the way of Jesus, a truth that cannot be supported by violence, a truth that violent enforcement can only contradict. That truth may also prove unsettling for secular society, for it certainly cannot leave society to go its own way unchallenged. But its power to disturb is part and parcel of its intrinsic power to convince.

(8) Truth in a Pluralistic World

For a Christian community to be faithful to the truth of the gospel it must be alert to the danger of coming to think that truth is something it possesses and can put to use. God's truth is not what works for us, not what we find useful, but what claims us and impels us always beyond our own concerns. God's truth is always greater than we imagine.

Christians are people who — while recognizing the transcendence of truth, that we can never grasp and possess it — do care about truth, and this enables them to engage seriously and respectfully in dialogue with people who think differently. It is not the relativists — who think every claim to truth as valid or as invalid as every other — who can participate with others in serious conversation about truth. Only if we think that error is a real possibility and idolatry a real temptation can we be serious about truth in a way that qualifies us to engage with others who care about truth.

The world is a complex place, and there are truths of all kinds to be found in all sorts of predictable and also quite unexpected places in it. If we want to claim, as I think we should, the universality and definitiveness of Jesus Christ as the key to all truth we need not think of this in a purely exclusionary way but can profitably consider it as relational truth. That is, all truth will come finally into its own, find its place in the still far from realized scheme of things, when it is brought into relationship with Jesus Christ. So just as witness to the truth of Jesus cannot be pursued by coercion and violence, so also it cannot be furthered by minds arrogantly or even fearfully closed to whatever truth there may be to be known. As those who belong to the truth of God in Jesus Christ, those who have been claimed by the truth of the gospel, we must above all be faithful to the truth that has claimed us, but, just because that truth claims universal relevance, just because it is not an unpretentious little local truth but the truth of God, we must go on seeking its relevance out there in the world with other seekers of truth.

Index of Modern Authors

Index of Modern Authors

Index of Scripture References

174

Index of Scripture References

INDEX OF SCRIPTURE REFERENCES